Bitcoin goes KABOOM!

Caveat Emptor – Let the Buyer Beware

William Peterson

Contents

Chapter 1 – Tulip Mania………….   pg 4-16

Chapter 2 – Bitcoin 101……………….   pg 17-54

Chapter 3 – World's Central Bankers…   pg 54-60

Chapter 4 – Gold 2.0………………….   pg 61-68

Chapter 5 – Fiat is Fiat is Fiat……….   pg 69-76

Chapter 6 – Bitcoin Booms and Busts…   pg 77-84

Chapter 7 – Perception vs. Reality……   pg 85-92

Chapter 8 – Libertarian Warning………   pg 93-103

Chapter 1 – Tulip Mania

This original story is from Charles Mackay's *"Extraordinary Popular Delusions and the Madness of Crowds"* written in 1841:

The tulip,-so named, it is said, from a Turkish word, signifying a turban,- was introduced into western Europe about the middle of the sixteenth century.

Conrad Gesner, who claims the merit of having brought it into repute,-little dreaming of the extraordinary commotion it was to make in the world,-says that he first saw it in the year 1559, in a garden at Augsburg, belonging to the learned Counsellor Herwart, a man very famous in his day for his collection of rare exotics.

The bulbs were sent to this gentleman by a friend at Constantinople, where the flower had long been a favourite.

In the course of ten or eleven years after this period, tulips were much sought after by the wealthy, especially in Holland and Germany. Rich people at Amsterdam sent for the bulbs direct to Constantinople, and paid the most extravagant prices for them.

The first roots planted in England were brought from Vienna in 1600. Until the year 1634 the tulip annually increased in reputation, until it was deemed a proof of bad taste in any man of fortune to be without a collection of them. Many learned men, including Pompeius de Angelis and the celebrated Lipsius of Leyden, the author of the treatise "De Constantia," were passionately fond of tulips.

The rage for possessing them soon caught the middle classes of society, and merchants and shopkeepers, even of moderate means, began to vie with each other in the rarity of these flowers and the preposterous prices they paid for them.

A trader at Harlaem was known to pay one-half of his fortune for a single root-not with the design of selling it again at a profit, but to keep in his own conservatory for the admiration of his acquaintance.

One would suppose that there must have been some great virtue in this flower to have made it so valuable in the eyes of so prudent a people as the Dutch; but it has neither the beauty nor the perfume of the rose-hardly the beauty of the "sweet, sweet-pea;" neither is it as enduring as either. Cowley, it is true, is loud in its praise. He says-

"The tulip next appeared, all over gay,
But wanton, full of pride, and full of play;
The world can't show a dye but here has place;
Nay, by new mixtures, she can change her face;
Purple and gold are both beneath her care-
The richest needlework she loves to wear;
Her only study is to please the eye,
And to outshine the rest in finery."

This, though not very poetical, is the description of a poet. Beckmann, in his History of Inventions, paints it with more fidelity, and in prose more pleasing than Cowley's poetry.

He says, "There are few plants which acquire, through accident, weakness, or disease, so many variegations as the tulip. When uncultivated, and in its natural state, it is almost of one colour, has large leaves, and an extraordinarily long stem. When it has been weakened by cultivation, it becomes more agreeable in the eyes of the florist. The petals are then paler, smaller, and more diversified in hue; and the leaves acquire a softer green colour. Thus this masterpiece of culture, the more beautiful it turns, grows so much the weaker, so that, with the greatest skill and most careful attention, it can scarcely be transplanted, or even kept alive."

Many persons grow insensibly attached to that which gives them a great deal of trouble, as a mother often loves her sick and ever-ailing child better than her more healthy offspring.

Upon the same principle we must account for the unmerited encomia lavished upon these fragile blossoms. In 1634, the rage among the Dutch to possess them was so great that the ordinary industry of the country was neglected, and the population, even to its lowest dregs, embarked in the tulip trade. As the mania increased, prices augmented, until, in the year 1635, many persons were known to invest a fortune of 100,000 florins in the purchase of forty roots.

It then became necessary to sell them by their weight in perits, a small weight less than a grain. A tulip of the species called Admiral Liefken, weighing 400 perits, was worth 4400 florins; an Admiral Von der Eyk, weighing 446 perits, was worth 1260 florins; a shilder of 106 perits was worth 1615 florins; a viceroy of 400 perits, 3000 florins, and, most precious of all, a Semper Augustus, weighing 200 perits, was thought to be very cheap at 5500 florins.

The latter was much sought after, and even an inferior bulb might command a price of 2000 florins. It is related that, at one time, early in 1636, there were only two roots of this description to be had in all Holland, and those not of the best.

One was in the possession of a dealer in Amsterdam, and the other in Harlaem. So anxious were the speculators to obtain them that one person offered the fee-simple of twelve acres of building ground for the Harlaem tulip. That of Amsterdam was bought for 4600 florins, a new carriage, two grey horses, and a complete suit of harness.

Munting, an industrious author of that day, who wrote a folio volume of one thousand pages upon the tulipomania, has preserved the following list of the various articles, and their value, which were delivered for one single root of the rare species called the viceroy:-

Item	Value (florins)
Two lasts of wheat	448
Four lasts of rye	558
Four fat oxen	480
Eight fat swine	240
Twelve fat sheep	120
Two hogsheads of wine	70
Four tuns of beer	32
Two tons of butter	192
A complete bed	100
A suit of clothes	80
A silver drinking cup	60
Total	**2,500**

People who had been absent from Holland, and whose chance it was to return when this folly was at its maximum, were sometimes led into awkward dilemmas by their ignorance. There is an amusing instance of the kind related in Blainville's Travels.

A wealthy merchant, who prided himself not a little on his rare tulips, received upon one occasion a very valuable consignment of merchandise from the Levant.

Intelligence of its arrival was brought him by a sailor, who presented himself for that purpose at the counting-house, among bales of goods of every description.

The merchant, to reward him for his news, munificently made him a present of a fine red herring for his breakfast. The sailor had, it appears, a great partiality for onions, and seeing a bulb very like an onion lying upon the counter of this liberal trader, and thinking it, no doubt, very much out of its place among silks and velvets, he slily seized an opportunity and slipped it into his pocket, as a relish for his herring. He got clear off with his prize, and proceeded to the quay to eat his breakfast. Hardly was his back turned when the merchant missed his valuable Semper Augustus, worth three thousand florins, or about 280 pounds sterling.

The whole establishment was instantly in an uproar; search was everywhere made for the precious root, but it was not to be found. Great was the merchant's distress of mind. The search was renewed, but again without success. At last some one thought of the sailor.

The unhappy merchant sprang into the street at the bare suggestion. His alarmed household followed him. The sailor, simple soul! had not thought of concealment. He was found quietly sitting on a coil of ropes, masticating the last morsel of his "onion." Little did he dream that he had been eating a breakfast whose cost might have regaled a whole ship's crew for a twelvemonth; or, as the plundered merchant himself expressed it, "might have sumptuously feasted the Prince of Orange and the whole court of the Stadtholder."

Anthony caused pearls to be dissolved in wine to drink the health of Cleopatra; Sir Richard Whittington was as foolishly magnificent in an entertainment to King Henry V; and Sir Thomas Gresham drank a diamond, dissolved in wine, to the health of Queen Elizabeth, when she opened the Royal Exchange: but the breakfast of this roguish Dutchman was as splendid as either. He had an advantage, too, over his wasteful predecessors: their gems did not improve the taste or the wholesomeness of their wine, while his tulip was quite delicious with his red herring.

The most unfortunate part of the business for him was, that he remained in prison for some months, on a charge of felony, preferred against him by the merchant.

Another story is told of an English traveller, which is scarcely less ludicrous. This gentleman, an amateur botanist, happened to see a tulip-root lying in the conservatory of a wealthy Dutchman.

Being ignorant of its quality, he took out his penknife, and peeled off its coats, with the view of making experiments upon it. When it was by this means reduced to half its original size, he cut it into two equal sections, making all the time many learned remarks on the singular appearances of the unknown bulb. Suddenly the owner pounced upon him, and, with fury in his eyes, asked him if he knew what he had been doing? "Peeling a most extraordinary onion," replied the philosopher. "Hundert tausend duyvel," said the Dutchman; "it's an Admiral Von der Eyk." "Thank you," replied the traveller, taking out his note-book to make a memorandum of the same; "are these admirals common in your country?"

"Death and the devil," said the Dutchman, seizing the astonished man of science by the collar; "come before the syndic, and you shall see." In spite of his remonstrances, the traveller was led through the streets, followed by a mob of persons.

When brought into the presence of the magistrate, he learned, to his consternation, that the root upon which he had been experimentalizing was worth four thousand florins; and, notwithstanding all he could urge in extenuation, he was lodged in prison until he found securities for the payment of this sum.

The demand for tulips of a rare species increased so much in the year 1636, that regular marts for their sale were established on the Stock Exchange of Amsterdam, in Rotterdam, Harlaem, Leyden, Alkmar, Hoorn, and other towns.

Symptoms of gambling now became, for the first time, apparent. The stockjobbers, ever on the alert for a new speculation, dealt largely in tulips, making use of all the means they so well knew how to employ, to cause fluctuations in prices.

At first, as in all these gambling mania, confidence was at its height, and everybody gained. The tulip-jobbers speculated in the rise and fall of the tulip stocks, and made large profits by buying when prices fell, and selling out when they rose. Many individuals grew suddenly rich. A golden bait hung temptingly out before the people, and, one after the other, they rushed to the tulip marts, like flies around a honeypot.

Every one imagined that the passion for tulips would last for ever, and that the wealthy from every part of the world would send to Holland, and pay whatever prices were asked for them.

The riches of Europe would be concentrated on the shores of the Zuyder Zee, and poverty banished from the favoured clime of Holland.

Nobles, citizens, farmers, mechanics, seamen, footmen, maidservants, even chimney-sweeps and old clotheswomen, dabbled in tulips. People of all grades converted their property into cash, and invested it in flowers. Houses and lands were offered for sale at ruinously low prices, or assigned in payment of bargains made at the tulip-mart.

Foreigners became smitten with the same frenzy, and money poured into Holland from all directions. The prices of the necessaries of life rose again by degrees; houses and lands, horses and carriages, and luxuries of every sort, rose in value with them, and for some months Holland seemed the very antechamber of Plutus. The operations of the trade became so extensive and so intricate, that it was found necessary to draw up a code of laws for the guidance of the dealers.

Notaries and clerks were also appointed, who devoted themselves exclusively to the interests of the trade. The designation of public notary was hardly known in some towns, that of tulip notary usurping its place. In the smaller towns, where there was no exchange, the principal tavern was usually selected as the "showplace," where high and low traded in tulips, and confirmed their bargains over sumptuous entertainments.

These dinners were sometimes attended by two or three hundred persons, and large vases of tulips, in full bloom, were placed at regular intervals upon the tables and sideboards, for their gratification during the repast.

At last, however, the more prudent began to see that this folly could not last for ever. Rich people no longer bought the flowers to keep them in their gardens, but to sell them again at cent. It was seen that somebody must lose fearfully in the end.

As this conviction spread, prices fell, and never rose again. Confidence was destroyed, and a universal panic seized upon the dealers. A had agreed to purchase ten Sempers Augustines from B, at four thousand florins each, at six weeks after the signing of the contract. B was ready with the flowers at the appointed time; but the price had fallen to three or four hundred florins, and A refused either to pay the difference or receive the tulips.

Defaulters were announced day after day in all the towns of Holland. Hundreds who, a few months previously, had begun to doubt that there was such a thing as poverty in the land, suddenly found themselves the possessors of a few bulbs, which nobody would buy, even though they offered them at one quarter of the sums they had paid for them.

The cry of distress resounded everywhere, and each man accused his neighbour. The few who had contrived to enrich themselves hid their wealth from the knowledge of their fellow-citizens, and invested it in the English or other funds.

Many who, for a brief season, had emerged from the humbler walks of life, were cast back into their original obscurity. Substantial merchants were reduced almost to beggary, and many a representative of a noble line saw the fortunes of his house ruined beyond redemption.

When the first alarm subsided, the tulip-holders in the several towns held public meetings to devise what measures were best to be taken to restore public credit. It was generally agreed, that deputies should be sent from all parts to Amsterdam, to consult with the government upon some remedy for the evil.

The Government at first refused to interfere, but advised the tulip-holders to agree to some plan among themselves. Several meetings were held for this purpose; but no measure could be devised likely to give satisfaction to the deluded people, or repair even a slight portion of the mischief that had been done.

The language of complaint and reproach was in everybody's mouth, and all the meetings were of the most stormy character. At last, however, after much bickering and ill-will, it was agreed, at Amsterdam, by the assembled deputies, that all contracts made in the height of the mania, or prior to the month of November 1636, should be declared null and void, and that, in those made after that date, purchasers should be freed from their engagements, on paying ten per cent. to the vendor.

This decision gave no satisfaction. The vendors who had their tulips on hand were, of course, discontented, and those who had pledged themselves to purchase, thought themselves hardly treated. Tulips which had, at one time, been worth six thousand florins, were now to be procured for five hundred; so that the composition of ten per cent. was one hundred florins more than the actual value.

Actions for breach of contract were threatened in all the courts of the country; but the latter refused to take cognizance of gambling transactions.

The matter was finally referred to the Provincial Council at the Hague, and it was confidently expected that the wisdom of this body would invent some measure by which credit should be restored.

Expectation was on the stretch for its decision, but it never came. The members continued to deliberate week after week, and at last, after thinking about it for three months, declared that they could offer no final decision until they had more information.

They advised, however, that, in the mean time, every vendor should, in the presence of witnesses, offer the tulips in natura to the purchaser for the sums agreed upon. If the latter refused to take them, they might be put up for sale by public auction, and the original contractor held responsible for the difference between the actual and the stipulated price. This was exactly the plan recommended by the deputies, and which was already shown to be of no avail.

There was no court in Holland which would enforce payment. The question was raised in Amsterdam, but the judges unanimously refused to interfere, on the ground that debts contracted in gambling were no debts in law.

Thus the matter rested. To find a remedy was beyond the power of the government. Those who were unlucky enough to have had stores of tulips on hand at the time of the sudden reaction were left to bear their ruin as philosophically as they could; those who had made profits were allowed to keep them; but the commerce of the country suffered a severe shock, from which it was many years ere it recovered.

The example of the Dutch was imitated to some extent in England. In the year 1636 tulips were publicly sold in the Exchange of London, and the jobbers exerted themselves to the utmost to raise them to the fictitious value they had acquired in Amsterdam.

In Paris also the jobbers strove to create a tulipomania. In both cities they only partially succeeded. However, the force of example brought the flowers into great favour, and amongst a certain class of people tulips have ever since been prized more highly than any other flowers of the field.

The Dutch are still notorious for their partiality to them, and continue to pay higher prices for them than any other people. As the rich Englishman boasts of his fine race-horses or his old pictures, so does the wealthy Dutchman vaunt him of his tulips.

In England, in our day, strange as it may appear, a tulip will produce more money than an oak. If one could be found, rara in tetris, and black as the black swan alluded to by Juvenal, its price would equal that of a dozen acres of standing corn.

In Scotland, towards the close of the seventeenth century, the highest price for tulips, according to the authority of a writer in the supplement to the third edition of the "Encyclopedia Britannica," was ten guineas. Their value appears to have diminished from that time till the year 1769, when the two most valuable species in England were the Don Quevedo and the Valentinier, the former of which was worth two guineas and the latter two guineas and a half. These prices appear to have been the minimum.

In the year 1800, a common price was fifteen guineas for a single bulb. In 1835, so foolish were the fanciers, that a bulb of the species called the Miss Fanny Kemble was sold by public auction in London for seventy-five pounds. Still more astonishing was the price of a tulip in the possession of a gardener in the King's Road, Chelsea. In his catalogues, it was labelled at two hundred guineas!

Thus a flower, which for beauty and perfume was surpassed by the abundant roses of the garden,-a nosegay of which might be purchased for a penny,-was priced at a sum which would have provided an industrious labourer and his family with food, and clothes, and lodging for six years!

Should chickweed and groundsel ever come into fashion, the wealthy would, no doubt, vie with each other in adorning their gardens with them, and paying the most extravagant prices for them. In so doing, they would hardly be more foolish than the admirers of tulips. The common prices for these flowers at the present time vary from five to fifteen guineas, according to the rarity of the species.

Chapter 2 – Bitcoin & Tulip Mania

Knowing the story of Tulip Mania can you see the parallels to the digital currency world of Bitcoin?

Tulip Mania revolved around tens, then hundreds, then thousands of people that put dreams of grandeur in place of practical reality.

According to the story, "As the mania increased, prices augmented, until, in the year 1635, many persons were known to invest a fortune of 100,000 florins in the purchase of forty roots."

40 roots of flowers for 100,000 florins??!?!?!

Let's do the math:

100,000 Florins/40 Roots of Flowers = 2,500 Florins per root

That is INSANITY!!!

Take a look at the chart on the next page to see how much 1 tulip root could purchase at the height of the market in 1637. (See Table 1.1)

Can you imagine paying over $11,000 in today's money simply to purchase a tulip root? Well, can you imagine paying over $1,200 – and currently rising – for a digital piece of money that is created out of thin air and has no intrinsic value?

Item	Value (Florins)	~ Value (US Dollar $)
Two lasts of wheat	448	~ $300
Four lasts of rye	558	~ $800
Four fat oxen	480	~ $2400
Eight fat swine	240	~ $2400
Twelve fat sheep	120	~ $2400
Two hogsheads of wine	70	~ $350
Four tuns of beer	32	~$160
Two tons of butter	192	~$980
A complete bed	100	~$1300
A suit of clothes	80	~$300
A silver drinking cup	60	~$250
Total	**2,500**	~$11,640

The Tulip Mania story is important on so many levels. It tells the story of the rich and how Tulips came in to the economy. It tells the story of the speculators and the dealers. It tells the story of the Average Joe citizen who gets left holding the bad deals at the end of the day when the government can't intervene.

In the global economy in 2013, there is another Tulip Mania happening right before our eyes. It's called Bitcoin.

Here's some information directly from Bitcoin.Org website:

Some things you need to know

If you are about to explore Bitcoin, there are a few things you should know. Bitcoin lets you exchange money in a different way than with usual banks. As such, you should take time to inform yourself before using Bitcoin for any serious transaction. Bitcoin should be treated with the same care as your regular wallet, or even more in some cases!

Securing your wallet

Like in real life, your wallet must be secured. Bitcoin makes it possible to transfer value anywhere in a very easy way and it allows you to be in control of your money. Such great features also come with great security concerns. At the same time, Bitcoin can provide very high levels of security if used correctly. Always remember that it is your responsibility to adopt good practices in order to protect your money. Read more about securing your wallet.

Bitcoin price is volatile

The price of a bitcoin can unpredictably increase or decrease over a short period of time due to its young economy, novel nature, and sometimes illiquid markets. Consequently, keeping your savings with Bitcoin is not recommended at this point. Bitcoin should be seen like a high risk asset, and you should never store money that you cannot afford to lose with Bitcoin. If you receive payments with Bitcoin, many service providers can convert them to your local currency.

Bitcoin payments are irreversible

Any transaction issued with Bitcoin cannot be reversed, they can only be refunded by the person receiving the funds. That means you should take care to do business with people and organizations you know and trust, or who have an established reputation. For their part, businesses need to keep control of the payment requests they are displaying to their customers. Bitcoin can detect typos and usually won't let you send money to an invalid address by mistake. Additional services might exist in the future to provide more choice and protection for the consumer.

Bitcoin is not anonymous

Some effort is required to protect your privacy with Bitcoin. All Bitcoin transactions are stored publicly and permanently on the network, which means anyone can see the balance and transactions of any Bitcoin address. However, the identity of the user behind an address remains unknown until information is revealed during a purchase or in other circumstances. This is one reason why Bitcoin addresses should only be used once. Always remember that it is your responsibility to adopt good practices in order to protect your privacy. Read more about protecting your privacy.

Instant transactions are less secure

A Bitcoin transaction is usually deployed within a few seconds and begins to be confirmed in the following 10 minutes. During that time, a transaction can be considered authentic but still reversible. Dishonest users could try to cheat. If you can't wait for a confirmation, asking for a small transaction fee or using a detection system for unsafe transactions can increase security. For larger amounts like 1000 US$, it makes sense to wait for 6 confirmations or more. Each confirmation exponentially decreases the risk of a reversed transaction.

Bitcoin is still experimental

Bitcoin is an experimental new currency that is in active development. Although it becomes less experimental as usage grows, you should keep in mind that Bitcoin is a new invention that is exploring ideas that have never been attempted before. As such, its future cannot be predicted by anyone.

Don't forget government taxes

Bitcoin is not an official currency. That said, most jurisdictions still require you to pay income, sales, payroll, and capital gains taxes on anything that has value, including Bitcoin.

With all that information disclosed from their own website, right in front of your own eyes, why would you even consider using Bitcoin?

Consider the headlines:

- Securing your wallet
- Instant transactions are less secure
- Bitcoin is still experimental
- Bitcoin is not anonymous
- Bitcoin payments are irreversible
- Bitcoin price is volatile

Now – consider this abstract by Satashi Nakamoto, the creator of the digital currency:

A purely peer-to-peer version of electronic cash would allow online payments to be sent directly from one party to another without going through a financial institution.

Digital signatures provide part of the solution, but the main benefits are lost if a trusted third party is still required to prevent double-spending.

We propose a solution to the double-spending problem using a peer-to-peer network. The network timestamps transactions by hashing them into an ongoing chain of hash-based proof-of-work, forming a record that cannot be changed without redoing the proof-of-work. The longest chain not only serves as proof of the sequence of events witnessed, but proof that it came from the largest pool of CPU power.

As long as a majority of CPU power is controlled by nodes that are not cooperating to attack the network, they'll generate the longest chain and outpace attackers. The network itself requires minimal structure. Messages are broadcast on a best effort basis, and nodes can leave and rejoin the network at will, accepting the longest proof-of-work chain as proof of what happened while they were gone.

After all of that information, here's a quick reference guide from Bitcoin.org as of 11/29/2013:

What is Bitcoin?

Bitcoin is a consensus network that enables a new payment system and a completely digital money. It is the first decentralized peer-to-peer payment network that is powered by its users with no central authority or middlemen. From a user perspective, Bitcoin is pretty much like cash for the Internet. Bitcoin can also be seen as the most prominent triple entry bookkeeping in existence.

Who created Bitcoin?

Bitcoin is the first implementation of a concept called "crypto-currency", which was first described in 1998 by Wei Dai on the cypherpunks mailing list, suggesting the idea of a new form of money that uses cryptography to control its creation and transactions, rather than a central authority. The first Bitcoin specification and proof of concept was published in 2009 in a cryptography mailing list by Satoshi Nakamoto. Satoshi left the project in late 2010 without revealing much about himself. The community has since grown exponentially with many developers working on Bitcoin.

Satoshi's anonymity often raised unjustified concerns, many of which are linked to misunderstanding of the open-source nature of Bitcoin. The Bitcoin protocol and software

are published openly and any developer around the world can review the code or make their own modified version of the Bitcoin software. Just like current developers, Satoshi's influence was limited to the changes he made being adopted by others and therefore he did not control Bitcoin. As such, the identity of Bitcoin's inventor is probably as relevant today as the identity of the person who invented paper.

Who controls the Bitcoin network?

Nobody owns the Bitcoin network much like no one owns the technology behind email. Bitcoin is controlled by all Bitcoin users around the world. While developers are improving the software, they can't force a change in the Bitcoin protocol because all users are free to choose what software and version they use. In order to stay compatible with each other, all users need to use software complying with the same rules. Bitcoin can only work correctly with a complete consensus among all users. Therefore, all users and developers have a strong incentive to protect this consensus.

How does Bitcoin work?

From a user perspective, Bitcoin is nothing more than a mobile app or computer program that provides a personal Bitcoin wallet and allows a user to send and receive bitcoins with them. This is how Bitcoin works for most users.

Behind the scenes, the Bitcoin network is sharing a public ledger called the "block chain". This ledger contains every transaction ever processed, allowing a user's computer to verify the validity of each transaction. The authenticity of each transaction is protected by digital signatures corresponding to the sending addresses, allowing all users to have full control over sending bitcoins from their own Bitcoin addresses. In addition, anyone can process transactions using the computing power of specialized hardware and earn a reward in bitcoins for this service. This is often called "mining".

Is Bitcoin really used by people?

Yes. There is a growing number of businesses and individuals using Bitcoin. This includes brick and mortar businesses like restaurants, apartments, law firms, and popular online services such as Namecheap, WordPress, Reddit and Flattr. While Bitcoin remains a relatively new phenomenon, it is growing fast. At the end of August 2013, the value of all bitcoins in circulation exceeded US$ 1.5 billion with millions of dollars worth of bitcoins exchanged daily.

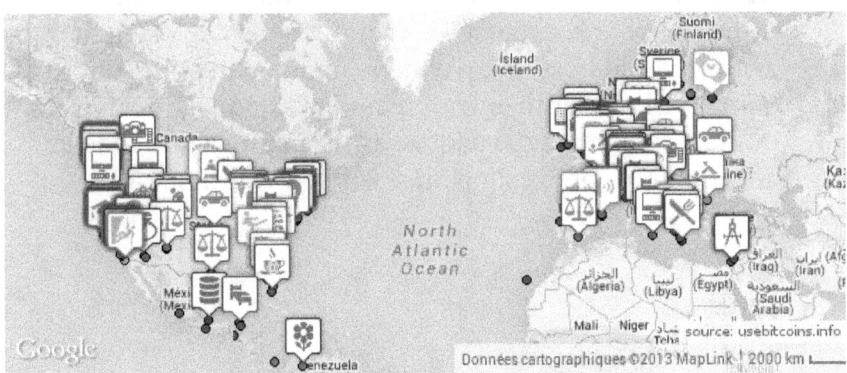

How does one acquire bitcoins?

- As payment for goods or services.
- Purchase bitcoins at a Bitcoin exchange.
- Exchange bitcoins with someone near you.
- Earn bitcoins through competitive mining.

While it may be possible to find individuals who wish to sell bitcoins in exchange for a credit card or PayPal payment, most exchanges do not allow funding via these payment methods. This is due to cases where someone buys bitcoins with PayPal, and then reverses their half of the transaction. This is commonly referred to as a chargeback.

How difficult is it to make a Bitcoin payment?

Bitcoin payments are easier to make than debit or credit card purchases, and can be received without a merchant account. Payments are made from a wallet application, either on your computer or smartphone, by entering the recipient's address, the payment amount, and pressing send. To make it easier to enter a recipient's address, many wallets can obtain the address by scanning a QR code or touching two phones together with NFC technology.

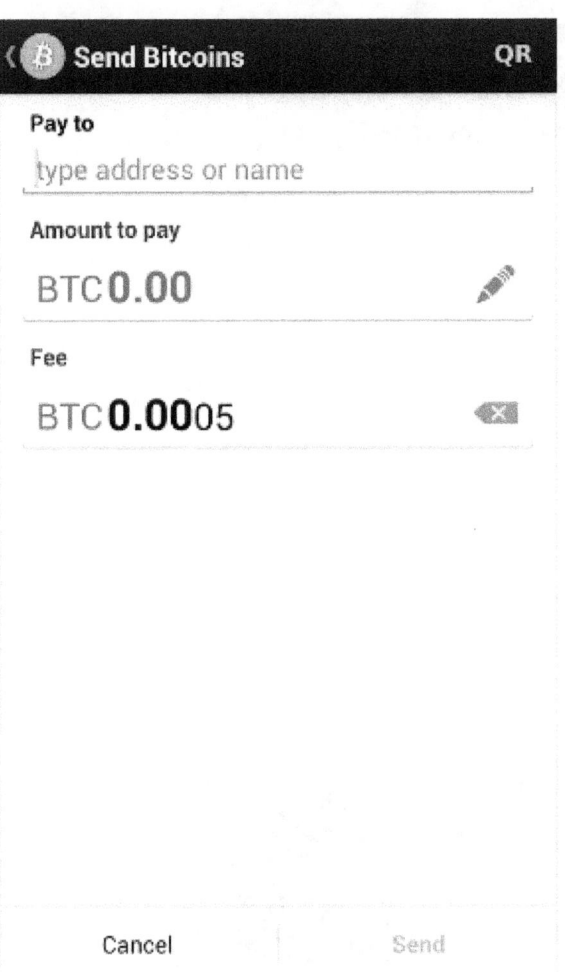

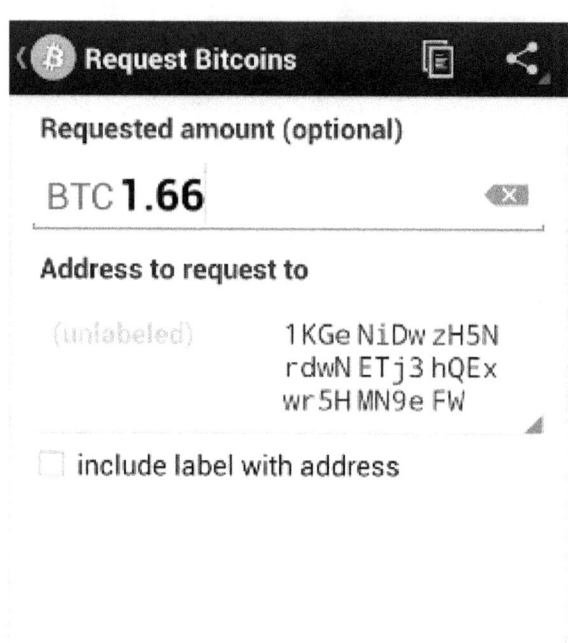

What are the advantages of Bitcoin?

- *Payment freedom* - It is possible to send and receive any amount of money instantly anywhere in the world at any time. No bank holidays. No borders. No imposed limits. Bitcoin allows its users to be in full control of their money.

- *Very low fees* - Bitcoin payments are currently processed with either no fees or extremely small fees. Users may include fees with transactions to receive priority processing, which results in faster confirmation of transactions by the network. Additionally, merchant processors exist to assist merchants in processing transactions, converting bitcoins to fiat currency and depositing funds directly into merchants' bank accounts daily. As these services are based on Bitcoin, they can be offered for much lower fees than with PayPal or credit card networks.

- *Fewer risks for merchants* - Bitcoin transactions are secure, irreversible, and do not contain customers' sensitive or personal information. This protects merchants from losses caused by fraud or fraudulent chargebacks, and there is no need for PCI compliance. Merchants can easily expand to new markets where either credit cards are not available or fraud rates are unacceptably high. The net results are lower fees, larger markets, and fewer administrative costs.

- ***Security and control*** - Bitcoin users are in full control of their transactions; it is impossible for merchants to force unwanted or unnoticed charges as can happen with other payment methods. Bitcoin payments can be made without personal information tied to the transaction. This offers strong protection against identity theft. Bitcoin users can also protect their money with backup and encryption.

- ***Transparent and neutral***: All information concerning the Bitcoin money supply itself is readily available on the block chain for anybody to verify and use in real-time. No individual or organization can control or manipulate the Bitcoin protocol because it is cryptographically secure. This allows the core of Bitcoin to be trusted for being completely neutral, transparent and predictable.

What are the disadvantages of Bitcoin?

- *Degree of acceptance* - Many people are still unaware of Bitcoin. Every day, more businesses accept bitcoins because they want the advantages of doing so, but the list remains small and still needs to grow in order to benefit from network effects.

- *Volatility* – The total value of bitcoins in circulation and the number of businesses using Bitcoin are still very small compared to what they could be. Therefore, relatively small events, trades, or business activities can significantly affect the price. In theory, this volatility will decrease as Bitcoin markets and the technology matures. Never before has the world seen a start-up currency, so it is truly difficult (and exciting) to imagine how it will play out.

- *Ongoing development* - Bitcoin software is still in beta with many incomplete features in active development. New tools, features, and services are being developed to make Bitcoin more secure and accessible to the masses. Some of these are still not ready for everyone. Most Bitcoin businesses are new and still offer no insurance. In general, Bitcoin is still in the process of maturing.

Why do people trust Bitcoin?

Much of the trust in Bitcoin comes from the fact that it requires no trust at all. Bitcoin is fully open-source and decentralized. This means that anyone has access to the entire source code at any time. Any developer in the world can therefore verify exactly how Bitcoin works. All transactions and bitcoins issued into existence can be transparently consulted in real-time by anyone. All payments can be made without reliance on a third party and the whole system is protected by heavily peer-reviewed cryptographic algorithms like those used for online banking. No organization or individual can control Bitcoin, and the network remains secure even if not all of its users can be trusted.

Can I make money with Bitcoin?

You should never expect to get rich with Bitcoin or any emerging technology. It is always important to be wary of anything that sounds too good to be true or disobeys basic economic rules.

Bitcoin is a growing space of innovation and there are business opportunities that also include risks. There is no guarantee that Bitcoin will continue to grow even though it has developed at a very fast rate so far. Investing time and resources on anything related to Bitcoin requires entrepreneurship. There are various ways to make money with Bitcoin such as mining, speculation or running new businesses. All of these methods are competitive and there is no guarantee of profit. It is up to each individual to make a proper evaluation of the costs and the risks involved in any such project.

Is Bitcoin fully virtual and immaterial?

Bitcoin is as virtual as the credit cards and online banking networks people use everyday. Bitcoin can be used to pay online and in physical stores just like any other form of money. Bitcoins can also be exchanged in physical form, such as the Casascius coins, but paying with a mobile phone usually remains more convenient. Bitcoin balances are stored in a large distributed network, and they cannot be fraudulently altered by anybody. In other words, Bitcoin users have exclusive control over their funds and bitcoins cannot vanish just because they are virtual.

Is Bitcoin anonymous?

Bitcoin is designed to allow its users to send and receive payments with an acceptable level of privacy as well as any other form of money. However, Bitcoin is not anonymous and cannot offer the same level of privacy as cash. The use of Bitcoin leaves extensive public records. Various mechanisms exist to protect users' privacy, and more are in development. However, there is still work to be done before these features are used correctly by most Bitcoin users.

Some concerns have been raised that private transactions could be used for illegal purposes with Bitcoin. However, it is worth noting that Bitcoin will undoubtedly be subjected to similar regulations that are already in place inside existing financial systems. Bitcoin cannot be more anonymous than cash and it is not likely to prevent criminal investigations from being conducted. Additionally, Bitcoin is also designed to prevent a large range of financial crimes.

What happens when bitcoins are lost?

When a user loses his wallet, it has the effect of removing money out of circulation. Lost bitcoins still remain in the block chain just like any other bitcoins. However, lost bitcoins remain dormant forever because there is no way for anybody to find the private key(s) that would allow them to be spent again. Because of the law of supply and demand, when fewer bitcoins are available, the ones that are left will be in higher demand and increase in value to compensate.

Can Bitcoin scale to become a major payment network?

The Bitcoin network can already process a much higher number of transactions per second than it does today. It is, however, not entirely ready to scale to the level of major credit card networks. Work is underway to lift current limitations, and future requirements are well known. Since inception, every aspect of the Bitcoin network has been in a continuous process of maturation, optimization, and specialization, and it should be expected to remain that way for some years to come. As traffic grows, more Bitcoin users may use lightweight clients, and full network nodes may become a more specialized service.

Legal

Is Bitcoin legal?

To the best of our knowledge, Bitcoin has not been made illegal by legislation in any jurisdiction. However, some jurisdictions (such as Argentina) severely restrict or ban all foreign currency. Other jurisdictions (such as Thailand) may limit the licensing of certain entities such as Bitcoin exchanges.

Regulators from various jurisdictions are taking steps to provide individuals and businesses with rules on how to integrate this new technology with the formal, regulated financial system. For example, the Financial Crimes Enforcement Network (FinCEN), a bureau in the United States Treasury Department, issued non-binding guidance on how it characterizes certain activities involving virtual currencies.

- Virtual Currency Schemes – European Central Bank
- Application of FinCEN's Regulations to Persons Administering, Exchanging, or Using Virtual Currencies.

Is Bitcoin useful for illegal activities?

Bitcoin is money, and money has always been used both for legal and illegal purposes. Cash, credit cards and current banking systems widely surpass Bitcoin in terms of their use to finance crime. Bitcoin can bring significant innovation in payment systems and the benefits of such innovation are often considered to be far beyond their potential drawbacks.

Bitcoin is designed to be a huge step forward in making money more secure and could also act as a significant protection against many forms of financial crime. For instance, bitcoins are completely impossible to counterfeit. Users are in full control of their payments and cannot receive unapproved charges such as with credit card fraud. Bitcoin transactions are irreversible and immune to fraudulent chargebacks. Bitcoin allows money to be secured against theft and loss using very strong and useful mechanisms such as backups, encryption, and multiple signatures.

Some concerns have been raised that Bitcoin could be more attractive to criminals because it can be used to make private and irreversible payments. However, these features already exist with cash and wire transfer, which are widely used and well-established. The use of Bitcoin will undoubtedly be subjected to similar regulations that are already in place inside existing financial systems, and Bitcoin is not likely to prevent criminal investigations from being conducted. In general, it is common for important breakthroughs to be perceived as being controversial before their benefits are well understood. The Internet is a good example among many others to illustrate this.

Can Bitcoin be regulated?

The Bitcoin protocol itself cannot be modified without the cooperation of nearly all its users, who choose what software they use. Attempting to assign special rights to a local authority in the rules of the global Bitcoin network is not a practical possibility. Any rich organization could choose to invest in mining hardware to control half of the computing power of the network and become able to block or reverse recent transactions. However, there is no guarantee that they could retain this power since this requires to invest as much than all other miners in the world.

It is however possible to regulate the use of Bitcoin in a similar way to any other instrument. Just like the dollar, Bitcoin can be used for a wide variety of purposes, some of which can be considered legitimate or not as per each jurisdiction's laws. In this regard, Bitcoin is no different than any other tool or resource and can be subjected to different regulations in each country. Bitcoin use could also be made difficult by restrictive regulations, in which case it is hard to determine what percentage of users would keep using the technology. A government that chooses to ban Bitcoin would prevent domestic businesses and markets from developing, shifting innovation to other countries. The challenge for regulators, as always, is to develop efficient solutions while not impairing the growth of new emerging markets and businesses.

What about Bitcoin and taxes?

Bitcoin is not a fiat currency with legal tender status in any jurisdiction, but often tax liability accrues regardless of the medium used. There is a wide variety of legislation in many different jurisdictions which could cause income, sales, payroll, capital gains, or some other form of tax liability to arise with Bitcoin.

What about Bitcoin and consumer protection?

Bitcoin is freeing people to transact on their own terms. Each user can send and receive payments in a similar way to cash but they can also take part in more complex contracts. Multiple signatures allow a transaction to be accepted by the network only if a certain number of a defined group of persons agree to sign the transaction. This allows innovative dispute mediation services to be developed in the future. Such services could allow a third party to approve or reject a transaction in case of disagreement between the other parties without having control on their money. As opposed to cash and other payment methods, Bitcoin always leave a public proof that a transaction did take place, which can potentially be used in a recourse against businesses with fraudulent practices.

It is also worth noting that while merchants usually depend on their public reputation to remain in business and pay their employees, they don't have access to the same level of information when dealing with new consumers. The way Bitcoin works allows both individuals and businesses to be protected against fraudulent chargebacks while giving the choice to the consumer to ask for more protection when they are not willing to trust a particular merchant.

Economy

How are bitcoins created?

New bitcoins are generated by a competitive and decentralized process called "mining". This process involves that individuals are rewarded by the network for their services. Bitcoin miners are processing transactions and securing the network using specialized hardware and are collecting new bitcoins in exchange.

The Bitcoin protocol is designed in such a way that new bitcoins are created at a fixed rate. This makes Bitcoin mining a very competitive business. When more miners join the network, it becomes increasingly difficult to make a profit and miners must seek efficiency to cut their operating costs. No central authority or developer has any power to control or manipulate the system to increase their profits. Every Bitcoin node in the world will reject anything that does not comply with the rules it expects the system to follow.

Bitcoins are created at a decreasing and predictable rate. The number of new bitcoins created each year is automatically halved over time until bitcoin issuance halts completely with a total of 21 million bitcoins in existence. At this point, Bitcoin miners will probably be supported exclusively by numerous small transaction fees.

Why do bitcoins have value?

Bitcoins have value because they are useful as a form of money. Bitcoin has the characteristics of money (durability, portability, fungibility, scarcity, divisibility, and recognizability) based on the properties of mathematics rather than relying on physical properties (like gold and silver) or trust in central authorities (like fiat currencies). In short, Bitcoin is backed by mathematics. With these attributes, all that is required for a form of money to hold value is trust and adoption. In the case of Bitcoin, this can be measured by its growing base of users, merchants, and startups. As with all currency, bitcoin's value comes only and directly from people willing to accept them as payment.

What determines bitcoin's price?

The price of a bitcoin is determined by supply and demand. When demand for bitcoins increases, the price increases, and when demand falls, the price falls. There is only a limited number of bitcoins in circulation and new bitcoins are created at a predictable and decreasing rate, which means that demand must follow this level of inflation to keep the price stable. Because Bitcoin is still a relatively small market compared to what it could be, it doesn't take significant amounts of money to move the market price up or down, and thus the price of a bitcoin is still very volatile.

Bitcoin price, 2011 to 2013:

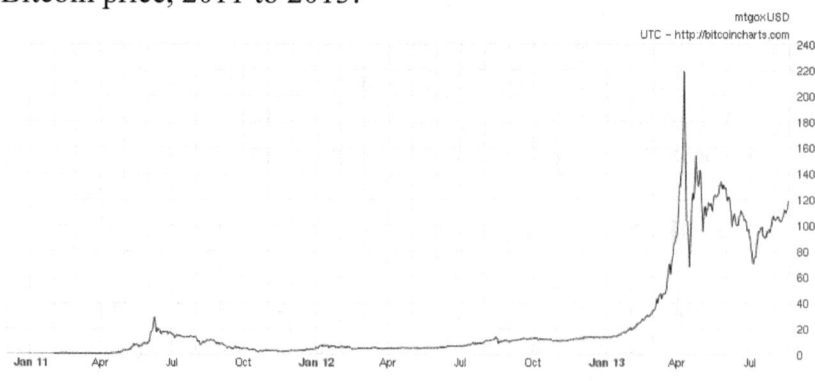

Can bitcoins become worthless?

Yes. History is littered with currencies that failed and are no longer used, such as the German Mark during the Weimar Republic and, more recently, the Zimbabwean dollar. Although previous currency failures were typically due to hyperinflation of a kind that Bitcoin makes impossible, there is always potential for technical failures, competing currencies, political issues and so on. As a basic rule of thumb, no currency should be considered absolutely safe from failures or hard times. Bitcoin has proven reliable for years since its inception and there is a lot of potential for Bitcoin to continue to grow. However, no one is in a position to predict what the future will be for Bitcoin.

Is Bitcoin a bubble?

A fast rise in price does not constitute a bubble. An artificial over-valuation that will lead to a sudden downward correction constitutes a bubble. Choices based on individual human action by hundreds of thousands of market participants is the cause for bitcoin's price to fluctuate as the market seeks price discovery. Reasons for changes in sentiment may include a loss of confidence in Bitcoin, a large difference between value and price not based on the fundamentals of the Bitcoin economy, increased press coverage stimulating speculative demand, fear of uncertainty, and old-fashioned irrational exuberance and greed.

Is Bitcoin a Ponzi scheme?

A Ponzi scheme is a fraudulent investment operation that pays returns to its investors from their own money, or the money paid by subsequent investors, instead of from profit earned by the individuals running the business. Ponzi schemes are designed to collapse at the expense of the last investors when there is not enough new participants.

Bitcoin is a free software project with no central authority. Consequently, no one is in a position to make fraudulent representations about investment returns. Like other major currencies such as gold, United States dollar, euro, yen, etc. there is no guaranteed purchasing power and the exchange rate floats freely. This leads to volatility where owners of bitcoins can unpredictably make or lose money. Beyond speculation, Bitcoin is also a payment system with useful and competitive attributes that are being used by thousands of users and businesses.

Doesn't Bitcoin unfairly benefit early adopters?

Some early adopters have large numbers of bitcoins because they took risks and invested time and resources in an unproven technology that was hardly used by anyone and that was much harder to secure properly. Many early adopters spent large numbers of bitcoins quite a few times before they became valuable or bought only small amounts and didn't make huge gains. There is no guarantee that the price of a bitcoin will increase or drop. This is very similar to investing in an early startup that can either gain value through its usefulness and popularity, or just never break through. Bitcoin is still in its infancy, and it has been designed with a very long-term view; it is hard to imagine how it could be less biased towards early adopters, and today's users may or may not be the early adopters of tomorrow.

Won't the finite amount of bitcoins be a limitation?

Bitcoin is unique in that only 21 million bitcoins will ever be created. However, this will never be a limitation because bitcoins can be divided up to 8 decimal places (0.000 000 01 BTC) and potentially even smaller units if that is ever required in the future. As the average transaction size decreases, transactions can be denominated in sub-units of a bitcoin, such as millibitcoins (1 mBTC or 0.001 BTC).

Won't Bitcoin fall in a deflationary spiral?

The deflationary spiral theory says that if prices are expected to fall, people will move purchases into the future in order to benefit from the lower prices. That fall in demand will in turn cause merchants to lower their prices to try and stimulate demand, making the problem worse and leading to an economic depression.

Although this theory is a popular way to justify inflation amongst central bankers, it does not appear to always hold true and is considered controversial amongst economists. Consumer electronics is one example of a market where prices constantly fall but which is not in depression. Similarly, the value of bitcoins has risen over time and yet the size of the Bitcoin economy has also grown dramatically along with it. Because both the value of the currency and the size of its economy started at zero in 2009, Bitcoin is a counterexample to the theory showing that it must sometimes be wrong.

Notwithstanding this, Bitcoin is not designed to be a deflationary currency. It is more accurate to say Bitcoin is intended to inflate in its early years, and become stable in its later years. The only time the quantity of bitcoins in circulation will drop is if people carelessly lose their wallets by failing to make backups. With a stable monetary base and a stable economy, the value of the currency should remain the same.

Isn't speculation and volatility a problem for Bitcoin?

This is a chicken and egg situation. For bitcoin's price to stabilize, a large scale economy needs to develop with more businesses and users. For a large scale economy to develop, businesses and users will seek for price stability.

Fortunately, volatility does not affect the main benefits of Bitcoin as a payment system to transfer money from point A to point B. It is possible for businesses to convert bitcoin payments to their local currency instantly, allowing them to profit from the advantages of Bitcoin without being subjected to price fluctuations. Since Bitcoin offers many useful and unique features and properties, many users choose to use Bitcoin. With such solutions and incentives, it is possible that Bitcoin will mature and develop to a degree where price volatility will become limited.

What if someone bought up all the existing bitcoins?

Only a fraction of bitcoins issued to date are found on the exchange markets for sale. Bitcoin markets are competitive, meaning the price of a bitcoin will rise or fall depending on supply and demand. Additionally, new bitcoins will continue to be issued for decades to come. Therefore even the most determined buyer could not buy all the bitcoins in existence. This situation isn't to suggest, however, that the markets aren't vulnerable to price manipulation; it still doesn't take significant amounts of money to move the market price up or down, and thus Bitcoin remains a volatile asset thus far.

What if someone creates a better digital currency?

That can happen. For now, Bitcoin remains by far the most popular decentralized virtual currency, but there can be no guarantee that it will retain that position. There is already a set of alternative currencies inspired by Bitcoin. It is however probably correct to assume that significant improvements would be required for a new currency to overtake Bitcoin in terms of established market, even though this remains unpredictable. Bitcoin could also conceivably adopt improvements of a competing currency so long as it doesn't change fundamental parts of the protocol.

Transactions

Why do I have to wait 10 minutes?

Receiving a payment is almost instant with Bitcoin. However, there is a 10 minutes delay on average before the network begins to confirm your transaction by including it in a block and before you can spend the bitcoins you receive. A confirmation means that there is a consensus on the network that the bitcoins you received haven't been sent to anyone else and are considered your property. Once your transaction has been included in one block, it will continue to be buried under every block after it, which will exponentially consolidate this consensus and decrease the risk of a reversed transaction. Every user is free to determine at what point they consider a transaction confirmed, but 6 confirmations is often considered to be as safe as waiting 6 months on a credit card transaction.

How much will the transaction fee be?

Most transactions can be processed without fees, but users are encouraged to pay a small voluntary fee for faster confirmation of their transactions and to remunerate miners. When fees are required, they generally don't exceed a few pennies in value. Your Bitcoin client will usually try to estimate an appropriate fee when required.

Transaction fees are used as a protection against users sending transactions to overload the network. The precise manner in which fees work is still being developed and will change over time. Because the fee is not related to the amount of bitcoins being sent, it may seem extremely low (0.0005 BTC for a 1,000 BTC transfer) or unfairly high (0.004 BTC for a 0.02 BTC payment). The fee is defined by attributes such as data in transaction and transaction recurrence. For example, if you are receiving a large number of tiny amounts, then fees for sending will be higher. Such payments are comparable to paying a restaurant bill using only pennies. Spending small fractions of your bitcoins rapidly may also require a fee. If your activity follows the pattern of conventional transactions, the fees should remain very low.

What if I receive a bitcoin when my computer is powered off?

This works fine. The bitcoins will appear next time you start your wallet application. Bitcoins are not actually received by the software on your computer, they are appended to a public ledger that is shared between all the devices on the network. If you are sent bitcoins when your wallet client program is not running and you later launch it, it will download blocks and catch up with any transactions it did not already know about, and the bitcoins will eventually appear as if they were just received in real time. Your wallet is only needed when you wish to spend bitcoins.

What does "synchronizing" mean and why does it take so long?

Long synchronization time is only required with full node clients like Bitcoin-Qt. Technically speaking, synchronizing is the process of downloading and verifying all previous Bitcoin transactions on the network. For some Bitcoin clients to calculate the spendable balance of your Bitcoin wallet and make new transactions, it needs to be aware of all previous transactions. This step can be resource intensive and requires sufficient bandwidth and storage to accommodate the full size of the block chain. For Bitcoin to remain secure, enough people should keep using full node clients because they perform the task of validating and relaying transactions.

Mining

What is Bitcoin mining?

Mining is the process of spending computing power to process transactions, secure the network, and keep everyone in the system synchronized together. It can be perceived like the Bitcoin data center except that it has been designed to be fully decentralized with miners operating in all countries and no individual having control over the network. This process is referred to as "mining" as an analogy to gold mining because it is also a temporary mechanism used to issue new bitcoins. Unlike gold mining, however, Bitcoin mining provides a reward in exchange for useful services required to operate a secure payment network. Mining will still be required after the last bitcoin is issued.

How does Bitcoin mining work?

Anybody can become a Bitcoin miner by running software with specialized hardware. Mining software listens for transactions broadcast through the peer-to-peer network and performs appropriate tasks to process and confirm these transactions. Bitcoin miners perform this work because they can earn transaction fees paid by users for faster transaction processing, and newly created bitcoins issued into existence according to a fixed formula.

For new transactions to be confirmed, they need to be included in a block along with a mathematical proof of work. Such proofs are very hard to generate because there is no way to create them other than by trying billions of calculations per second. This requires miners to perform these calculations before their blocks are accepted by the network and before they are rewarded. As more people start to mine, the difficulty of finding valid blocks is automatically increased by the network to ensure that the average time to find a block remains equal to 10 minutes. As a result, mining is a very competitive business where no individual miner can control what is included in the block chain.

The proof of work is also designed to depend on the previous block to force a chronological order in the block chain. This makes it exponentially difficult to reverse previous transactions because this requires the recalculation of the proofs of work of all the subsequent blocks. When two blocks are found at the same time, miners work on the first block they receive and switch to the longest chain of blocks as soon as the next block is found. This allows mining to secure and maintain a global consensus based on processing power.

Bitcoin miners are neither able to cheat by increasing their own reward nor process fraudulent transactions that could corrupt the Bitcoin network because all Bitcoin nodes would reject any block that contains invalid data as per the rules of the Bitcoin protocol. Consequently, the network remains secure even if not all Bitcoin miners can be trusted.

Isn't Bitcoin mining a waste of energy?

Spending energy to secure and operate a payment system is hardly a waste. Like any other payment service, the use of Bitcoin entails processing costs. Services necessary for the operation of currently widespread monetary systems, such as banks, credit cards, and armored vehicles, also use a lot of energy. Although unlike Bitcoin, their total energy consumption is not transparent and cannot be as easily measured.

Bitcoin mining has been designed to become more optimized over time with specialized hardware consuming less energy, and the operating costs of mining should continue to be proportional to demand. When Bitcoin mining becomes too competitive and less profitable, some miners choose to stop their activities. Furthermore, all energy expended mining is eventually transformed into heat, and the most profitable miners will be those who have put this heat to good use. An optimally efficient mining network is one that isn't actually consuming any extra energy. While this is an ideal, the economics of mining are such that miners individually strive toward it.

How does mining help secure Bitcoin?

Mining creates the equivalent of a competitive lottery that makes it very difficult for anyone to consecutively add new blocks of transactions into the block chain. This protects the neutrality of the network by preventing any individual from gaining the power to block certain transactions. This also prevents any individual from replacing parts of the block chain to roll back their own spends, which could be used to defraud other users. Mining makes it exponentially more difficult to reverse a past transaction by requiring the rewriting of all blocks following this transaction.

What do I need to start mining?

In the early days of Bitcoin, anyone could find a new block using their computer's CPU. As more and more people started mining, the difficulty of finding new blocks increased greatly to the point where the only cost-effective method of mining today is using specialized hardware.

Security

Is Bitcoin secure?

The Bitcoin technology - the protocol and the cryptography - has a strong security track record, and the Bitcoin network is probably the biggest distributed computing project in the world. Bitcoin's most common vulnerability is in user error. Bitcoin wallet files that store the necessary private keys can be accidentally deleted, lost or stolen. This is pretty similar to physical cash stored in a digital form. Fortunately, users can employ sound security practices to protect their money or use service providers that offer good levels of security and insurance against theft or loss.

Hasn't Bitcoin been hacked in the past?

The rules of the protocol and the cryptography used for Bitcoin are still working years after its inception, which is a good indication that the concept is well designed. However, security flaws have been found and fixed over time in various software implementations. Like any other form of software, the security of Bitcoin software depends on the speed with which problems are found and fixed. The more such issues are discovered, the more Bitcoin is gaining maturity.

There are often misconceptions about thefts and security breaches that happened on diverse exchanges and businesses. Although these events are unfortunate, none of them involve Bitcoin itself being hacked, nor imply inherent flaws in Bitcoin; just like a bank robbery doesn't mean that the dollar is compromised. However, it is accurate to say that a complete set of good practices and intuitive security solutions is needed to give users better protection of their money, and to reduce the general risk of theft and loss. Over the course of the last few years, such security features have quickly developed, such as wallet encryption, offline wallets, hardware wallets, and multi-signature transactions.

Could users collude against Bitcoin?

It is not possible to change the Bitcoin protocol that easily. Any Bitcoin client that doesn't comply with the same rules cannot enforce their own rules on other users. As per the current specification, double spending is not possible on the same block chain, and neither is spending bitcoins without a valid signature. Therefore, It is not possible to generate uncontrolled amounts of bitcoins out of thin air, spend other users' funds, corrupt the network, or anything similar.

However, a majority of miners could arbitrarily choose to block or reverse recent transactions. A majority of users can also put pressure for some changes to be adopted. Because Bitcoin only works correctly with a complete consensus between all users, changing the protocol can be very difficult and requires an overwhelming majority of users to adopt the changes in such a way that remaining users have nearly no choice but to follow. As a general rule, it is hard to imagine why any Bitcoin user would choose to adopt any change that could compromise their own money.

Is Bitcoin vulnerable to quantum computing?

Yes, most systems relying on cryptography in general are, including traditional banking systems. However, quantum computers don't yet exist and probably won't for a while. In the event that quantum computing could be an imminent threat to Bitcoin, the protocol could be upgraded to use post-quantum algorithms. Given the importance that this update would have, it can be safely expected that it would be highly reviewed by developers and adopted by all Bitcoin users.

Legal Disclaimer

This website provides information and material of a general nature. This information is intended for informational purposes only. This website may contain information that addresses real or potential legal issues. This information is not a substitute for qualified legal counsel. You are not authorized and nor should you rely on this website for legal advice. In no way are the owners of, or contributors to, this website responsible for the actions, decisions, or other behavior taken or not taken by you in reliance upon this website. This includes but is not limited to legal or technological reasons. You act at your own risk in reliance on the contents of this website. Should you make a decision to act or not act you should contact a licensed attorney in the relevant jurisdiction in which you want or need help.

This website may contain translations of the English version of content. These translations are provided only as a convenience. In the event of any conflict between the English language version and the translation version of content, the English language version takes precedence.

(http://bitcoin.org/en/)

Chapter 3 – World's Central Bankers

As one can see from all the Bitcoin information given in Chapter 2, in theory it seems like a grand idea for Bitcoins to flourish in today's society.

After all, there's only going to be 21,000,000 Bitcoins in existence at any one time. The structure is set up so mathematically it can't get any higher. Of course, structures change – especially when the world's central bankers get involved.

We've already seen the massive amounts of inflation and deflation in the US Dollar over the past 100 years. The United States dollar has been compromised ever since the Bretton Woods agreement of 1971. Some would argue the United States dollar has been compromised ever since the Federal Reserve came into existence.

There is always grave concern when the world's largest puppeteers – the central bankers – get together to determine "what money is" and "how it is valued."

Here are some quotes by some of the world's most powerful bankers concerning Bitcoin:

The People's Bank of China – Yi Gang

According to the Wall Street Journal, dated November 11, 2013 – Yi Gang responded to a question about Bitcoin at a financial seminar:

"What I can tell you now is that from the perspective of the People's Bank of China, for now we can't recognize [the legality] of the Bitcoin. But if you're interested, you can go ahead and do your research. You can go 'mining' and you can go to one of the exchanges. But if you want to take the risk—and remember that prices rise and fall – it's your business."

European Central Bank – Mario Draghi

On Gold:

It's *"fairly good protection against fluctuation of the Dollar and risk diversification. Central banks which had started a program of selling gold a few years ago substantially stopped; by and large they are not selling any longer. Also the experience of some central banks that have liquidated the whole stock about ten years ago was not considered to be terribly successful from a purely money viewpoint."*

(Source: "Central banks are unwise to sell their gold: ECB president Mario Draghi," Mining.com, October 17, 2013.)

Federal Reserve Board of Governors – Ben Bernanke

Ben Bernanke - United States Federal Reserve Board Chairman

"Historically, virtual currencies have been viewed as a form of "electronic money" or area of payment system technology that has been evolving over the past 20 years. Over time, these types of innovations have received attention from Congress as well as U.S. regulators. For example, in 1995, the U.S. House of Representatives held hearings on "the future of money" at which early versions of virtual currencies and other innovations were discussed. Vice Chairman Alan Blinder's testimony at that time made the key point that while these types of innovations may pose risks related to law enforcement and supervisory matters, there are also areas in which they may hold long-term promise, particularly if the innovations promote a faster, more secure and more efficient payment system."

Ben Bernanke, November 19, 2013

(Source: http://www.mining.com/ben-bernanke-comments-on-bitcoin-19316/)

Central Bank Russian Federation – Elvira Nabiullina

"The central bank isn't simply a commercial bank, it is above all the regulator of our financial system and the most powerful institution responsible for state economic policy."

"We don't need high short- term growth rates. We need steady and consistent growth that is mainly the result of greater efficiency, higher productivity and economic diversity. This is the main objective of the Central Bank's monetary policy."

"This time in Washington, attention was strongly focused on the consequences of a longer QE3, which could in fact lead to more economic bubbles and other system-wide risks. Of course, it is a complicated issue. Withdrawing too soon could be just as adverse as withdrawing too late. In any case, it is obvious – and all the participants mentioned this – that as the economy grows and recovers, the country should go back to more traditional monetary policy measures." – Elvira Naiullina, October 21, 2013

(Source: http://forexmagnates.com/russia-fx-regulatory-reform-continues-as-cbr-takes-over-new-role-as-financial-markets-watchdog/)

It's been obvious that the world's central bankers are at a loss with what to do about Bitcoin. Let's summarize the banker's statements in easy to read language:

Yi Gang, China – "Hey, if you want to purchase a digital currency that was created out of thin air – go for it. It's going up now – but beware, it might not be worth jack squat. If you want to gamble, that's your choice."

Mario Draghi, Europe – "Gold is a sensible way to protect your assets. Banks and bankers that have sold gold over the past 10 years have basically lost money."

Ben Bernanke, United States – "Electronic money is no different than what the Federal Reserve is already doing. We create and manipulate the value of the dollar on a daily basis. Maybe Bitcoin can do it better than we can – if it promotes a faster and more secure payment system."

Elvira Naiullina, Russia – "The Russia Central Bank is the holding tank for the whole economic system of Russia. Everything runs through us. We expect to manipulate the value of money how we see fit. Washington can keep screwing over everyone with QE3 – but we are hoping to get back to traditional monetary policy."

There you have 4 very different views on "money" and each of these men is designated leaders of their countries' economies. Some would argue that they are the most powerful and influential human beings alive on the planet Earth at this time!

Bitcoin enthusiasts would counter any argument of the World's Central Bankers by saying, "Hey – we're regulated by our own and we don't need a central bank telling us what to do anyway."

Bitcoins premise and desire to remove the central banks authority is valid and shows promise. The only problem is that Bitcoins do not hold any intrinsic and/or physical value. In that regard, Bitcoin is no different than imaginary money floating in the minds of the believers.

Chapter 4 – Gold 2.0

Countless articles are posted on the internet about Bitcoin as the new Gold 2.0. These articles tout the merits of Bitcoin and how they are so valuable. Right now, Bitcoins are only valuable because online retailers and some stores are accepting Bitcoins as a form of payment. What would happen if those stores/merchants decided not to accept Bitcoin?

Remember how the Tulip Mania got started? A few rich merchants decided to put an emphasis on the value of tulips, and 20 years later there was a huge run on tulips… and then KABOOM! The market crashed.

Check out this graph on Bitcoin value vs. the US Dollar from 2008 until now:

(See next page – Table 2.1)

B

Look at the major fluctuations Bitcoin has already gone thru!

On November 29, 2013, Bitcoin hit a "value" of $1,214 US Dollars!

On October 1, 2013, Bitcoin had a value of $140.30.

In April of 2013, Bitcoin had a value of $230.

In July of 2013, Bitcoin had a value of $70.

It's boom and bust, up and down – like the world's most terrifying roller coaster. Where will it all end up?

According to an article in the Economist, dated November 30, 2013, Bitcoin is facing quite a few problems:

(Source: http://www.economist.com/news/technology-quarterly/21590766-virtual-currency-it-mathematically-elegant-increasingly-popular-and-highly)

ALL currencies involve some measure of consensual hallucination, but Bitcoin, a virtual monetary system, involves more than most. It is a peer-to-peer currency with no central bank, based on digital tokens with no intrinsic value. Rather than relying on confidence in a central authority, it depends instead on a distributed system of trust, based on a transaction ledger which is cryptographically verified and jointly maintained by the currency's users.

Investors are backing Bitcoin-related startups, the German finance ministry has recognised it as a "unit of account" and senior officials told an American Senate committee on November 18th that virtual currencies had legitimate uses. But there have also been many cases of Bitcoin theft. Exchanges that convert Bitcoin to other currencies have collapsed or closed. Silk Road, an online forum where illicit goods and services are traded for Bitcoin, was shut down by America's Federal Bureau of Investigation in October 2013 but has since reopened. The Bitcoin price has fluctuated wildly, hitting $230 in April 2013, falling below $70 in July, and then exceeding $600 in November, prompting talk of a bubble.

The system is now straining at the seams. Its computational underpinnings have collectively reached 100 times the performance of the world's top 500 supercomputers combined: more than 50,000 petaflops. Bitcoin's success has revealed three weaknesses in particular. It is not as secure and anonymous as it seems; the "mining" system that both increases the Bitcoin supply and ensures the integrity of the currency has led to an unsustainable computational arms-race; and the distributed-ledger system is becoming unwieldy. Will Bitcoin's self-correcting mechanisms, and the enlightened self-interest of its users, be able to address these weaknesses and keep Bitcoin on the rails?

Bitcoin's growing popularity is having other ripple effects. Every participant in the system must keep a copy of the block chain, which now exceeds 11 gigabytes in size and continues to grow steadily. This alone deters casual use. Bitcoin's designer proposed a method of pruning the chain to include only unspent amounts, but it has not been implemented.

As the rate of transactions increases, squeezing all financial activity into the preset size limit for each block has started to become problematic. The protocol may need to be tweaked to allow more transactions per block, among other changes. A further problem relates to the volunteer machines, or nodes, that allow Bitcoin to function. These nodes relay transactions and transmit updates to the block chain. But, says Matthew Green, a security researcher at Johns Hopkins University, the ecosystem provides no compensation for maintaining these nodes—only for mining. The rising cost of operating nodes could jeopardise Bitcoin's ability to scale.

"The volunteer programmers who work on Bitcoin's software have no special authority in the system."

The original paper that sparked the creation of Bitcoin has since been supplemented by layers of agreed-upon protocol, updated regularly by the system's participants. The protocol, like the currency, is a fiction they accept as real, because rejection by a large proportion of users—be they banks, exchanges, speculators or miners—could cause the whole system to collapse. Mr Hearn notes that he and other programmers who work on Bitcoin's software have no special authority in the system. Instead, proposals are floated, implemented in software, and must then be taken up by 80% of nodes before becoming permanent—at which point blocks from other nodes are rejected. "The rules of the system are not set in stone," he says. The adoption of improvements is up to the community. Bitcoin is thus both flexible and fragile.

So far, it has kept going. But can it withstand the pressure as it becomes more popular? "It's got this kind of watch-like feel to it," says Mr Hearn. It keeps on ticking, but "a mechanical watch is fragile and can be smashed." Perhaps Bitcoin, like the internet, will smoothly evolve from a quirky experiment to a trusted utility. But it could also go the way of Napster, the trailblazing music-sharing system that pioneered a new category, but was superseded by superior implementations that overcame its technical and commercial flaws.

(Source: http://www.economist.com/news/technology-quarterly/21590766-virtual-currency-it-mathematically-elegant-increasingly-popular-and-highly)

Let's focus on some key points here:

Bitcoin is like a mechanical watch, "a mechanical watch is fragile and can be smashed."

Mechanical watches stop ticking at some point too…

"Volunteer programmers who work on Bitcoin's software have no special authority in the system."

It's like a house of cards. It just takes one person in the Bitcoin system to pull out without finding a replacement and the cards start falling.

"The rules of the system are not set in stone."

Bitcoin wants to create a self-reliant, self-sustaining monetary system that is controlled by market forces. Again – the idea is fantastic! The implementation is destined to fail.

Every participant in the system must keep a copy of the block chain, which now exceed 11 gigabytes in size and continues to grow steadily.

Can you imagine having to carry a $20 bill in your wallet that is over 1 mile long? How many times will you have to fold that over? Apply that analogy to the Bitcoin.

Here's an analysis of "GOLD 2.0" that was on MSNBC's Squawk Box, Tuesday, November 12, 2013:

(Source: http://www.cnbc.com/id/101192216)

The Winklevoss twins may say that bitcoin resembles "gold 2.0," but CEO of Euro Pacific Capital and Peter Schiff says the somewhat mysterious online currency more closely resembles tulip mania 2.0.

"A bubble is a bubble," he said. "And there's a bubble in bitcoins."

Schiff was responding to comments made by Tyler and Cameron Winklevoss, who have invested a great deal in bitcoins and are attempting to start a bitcoin exchange-traded fund. (They also happen to be well-known for suing Mark Zuckerberg over the creation of Facebook.)

On Tuesday's "Squawk Box," Cameron Winklevoss said that "some definitely view it as gold 2.0," adding, "In terms of a store of value, it definitely has the properties of gold, and people are viewing it that way."

But on the Tuesday episode of "Futures Now." Schiff, a longtime investor in gold, literally laughed at the comparison.

"I don't see bitcoins as an alternative to gold," he said. "If anything, [the creators of bitcoin are] modern-day alchemists, but you can't make gold digitally. It's no better than a fiat currency."

Schiff said that what he does see in the peer-to-peer currency—whose value has risen from $13.50 in January to $375 on Tuesday—is a bubble.

Discussing everything bitcoin—including how it works, its value and potential competitors—with Tyler and Cameron Winklevoss of Winklevoss Capital.

"To me, it looks like a modern-day tulip mania," Schiff said, referring to the fantastic rise and fall of the value of tulip bulbs in 17th-century Holland. "The reason people are buying bitcoins is because they think they're going to make money. They think the price is going up. And the price probably will go up. It'll keep going up until it implodes. And a lot of people are going to lose a lot of money in bitcoins."

Schiff scoffs at the idea that the bitcoin will become a common unit of online exchange.

"I don't think it's going to end up being a source of commerce for the world," he said. "I think right now it's a source of gambling."

But while Schiff is confident that bitcoins are in a bubble, he does have a major caveat.

"I don't know where the top is. Whether we're at the end now, or whether it will keep going on for months or years, I don't know," he said. "I mean, you can play the game if you want."

(Source: http://www.cnbc.com/id/101192216)

Chapter 5 – Fiat is Fiat is Fiat

For hundreds of years in human history, money has been the constant variable. If money truly is just a "means of exchange" – then why not just go create your own type of Bitcoin?

You can call it the Schmeely Coin or the Ruggerjup or any other silly name you can think of. You can get a couple of your Schmeely Coin friends to start the money and exchange it between one another. Then you could start to invite more friends into the Schmeely Coin and see if they want to invite more of their friends. If you have a viral money movement, and all your friends continue to use a Schmeely Coin in perpetuity then, CONGRATULATIONS, you have your own successful currency.

However, what happens if:

- Jason refuses payment of a Schmeely Coin from Jessica simply because he is angry with her?

- 7 Schmeely Coin Board of Governors join forces to undercut the value of the Schmeely Coin by creating thousands of new Schmeely Coins that flood the market?

- Ronald gives a Schmeely Coin to a friend for buying him lunch. Joe, Ronald's friend, decides to take that same Schmeely Coin and deposit it in the Schmeely Coin bank and the bank manager says, "Gee Joe, this is a fake Schmeely Coin."

All of those scenarios described would create huge waves of worry and panic in the Schmeely Coin value. Why would Bitcoin be any different?

The parallels are the same in the United States and the same problems are true for Central Banker's around the world. Money is FAKE. Fiat. It has no intrinsic value. It only has the worth of what the holder's of the money think it's worth.

When the FED decides to take Quantitative Easing to the next level and floods the market with easy money – what happens to the value of the dollar that is currently being held by savers? It decreases in value. It loses purchasing power.

Money is debt. If everyone in the world paid off their debts today and no credit was extended, the monetary system would simply implode.

In today's economic picture, countries are racing to devalue their currency. Why would any sane person want the purchasing power of his/her hard earned money to be less?

Countries do this so they can get a competitive advantage for imports and exports. It all revolves around trade.

For example, if the Japanese Yen and the US Dollar are both equal, say 1 to 1, then the cost of Toyota (a famous Japanese car maker) to produce a Toyota Camry is compared apples to apples with say an American car maker, Ford.

However, if the Japanese Yen is devalued – and $1 US Dollar is worth $1.20 Yen, then the Japanese have an advantage of how much money they bring into their country domestically. They earn more profit in "Yen".

So now, in today's global economy, you have countries that are racing to devalue their currency so they can have economic advantages with their own country. This race to devalue is called, "Currency Wars."

Cheaper currency boosts exports

A weak currency supports a country's exports by making its goods and services cheaper on the international market. A number of countries have therefore either allowed or encouraged their currency to depreciate this year.

The Japanese yen has fallen by more than 15% against the US dollar since the start of 2013. The country's central bank, the Bank of Japan, has done nothing to prevent its fall and, as a result, Japanese exports are steadily rising. In October 2013, Japan's exports leaped 18.6% from October 2012, marking their fastest year-on-year gain for three years.

Expectations that the Federal Reserve will soon start reducing – or 'tapering' – its so-called quantitative easing monetary stimulus has cause the Indian rupee to depreciate more than 20% against the US dollar since the beginning of this year.

The country's central bank, the Reserve Bank of India, initially panicked and intervened to support the rupee by selling dollars. But then it decided that a weaker rupee would benefit its sagging exports and allowed the currency to fall. Indian exports have since strengthened, jumping 12.97% in August 2013 – the fastest year-on-year growth for two years.

The Czech National Bank also recently intervened heavily to hold the Czech koruna down against the dollar and the euro. This was the first time in eleven years that the country's central bank had intervened in the currency market. It said that intervention was necessary in order to boost the Czech economy by driving up exports.

Fiat is Fiat is Fiat!!

Monetary policy is dictated by Bank "Boards of Governors" and Bank "Chairman" because the actual money they are using is FAKE.

Why do you think there is such a rush in speculation when ECB President Mario Draghi speaks? Or when Federal Reserve Chairman Ben Bernanke speaks?

These men – thru the power of their money printing machines – can dictate the value and purchasing power of your hard earned currency. How jacked up is that?

In this book, examples have been shown of how Bitcoin is a problem. It has no intrinsic value. The crazy part of this whole thing is that your paper dollar has no intrinsic value either!

Money used to be tied to gold because gold has a standard of weights and measures that can not be manipulated. 1 gram is 1 gram.

However, in today's monetary world, your dollar can shift in value at the whim of the central banking elite.

Bitcoin is using that knowledge to exploit a hole in the system. The problem is, Bitcoin has no intrinsic value, and rendered worthless if the crowds render it worthless.

Bitcoin does have some advantages

As Robert Tracinski, author of the individualist Tracinski Letter, put it:

"By creating something that has the basic characteristics of fiat currency, but which cannot be debased on whim, [the Bitcoin] tests the value of having a currency of limited quantity.

Or, to put things differently: it tests the destructiveness of having an unlimited quantity of money, as in the prevailing central banking system.

The extent to which investors and purchasers flee into the limited fiat money of Bitcoin is the extent to which they are fleeing out of the unlimited fiat money which our central bankers are vigorously debasing."

Bitcoin a true currency?

The only true currency? There is no difference between a dollar and a Bitcoin. They both backed by "confidence", not by anything real. The only reason why people want to buy Bitcoins is because they are rising in value.

If they were falling, very few people would use Bitcoin. Are you going put your hard worked money into something that loses value?

Why is Bitcoin rising? Simple, there are more buyers than sellers. Basically, the amount of bitcoins in circulation is very small. Look at the exchanges, and you will see that. People just accumulate Bitcoins. Why? Well, with the hope that it keeps rising. The moment all those buyers turn into sellers, you will see bitcoins smashed.

Million Dollar Question

Now folks, here's the million dollar question: "Which is better – a fake fiat currency that cannot be debased on a whim, or, a fake fiat currency that can be debased on a whim according to the overlords of the central banks?"

Either way – Fiat is Fiat is Fiat! There's no getting around it. Fake is Fake is Fake! While Bitcoin takes the "what is money" market for a ride, it's likely to end in Tulip Mania depression for those that choose to participate in it.

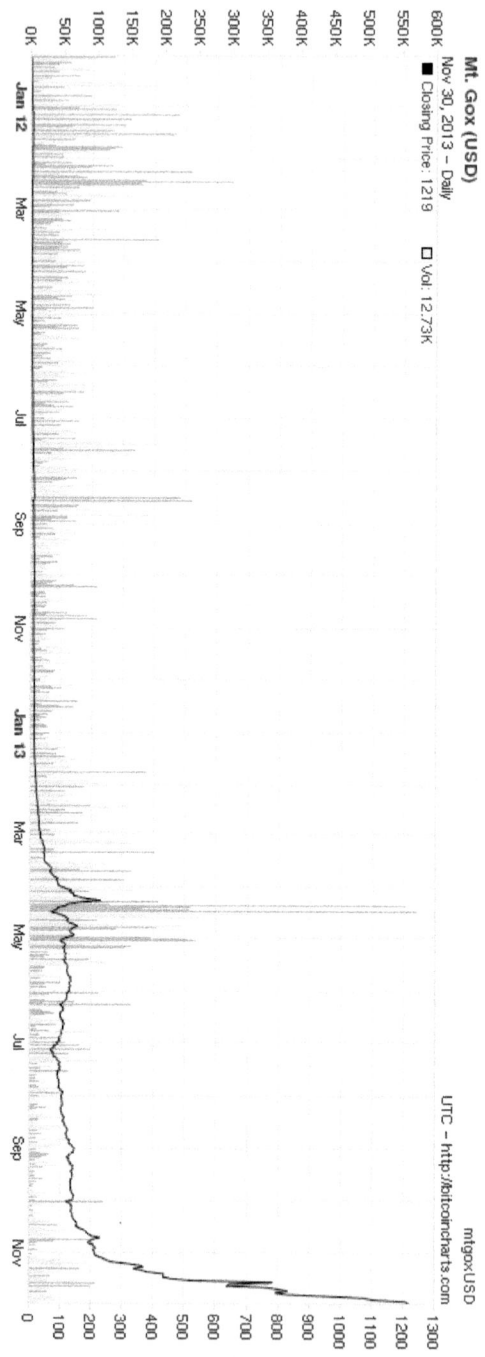

Chapter 6 – Bitcoin Booms & Busts

"Bitcoin is a very unique, unbelievably attractive form of money, currency. It has the benefit as operating as a medium of exchange. It's legal." – Jerry Robinson, economist.

Robinson also noted that he was introduced to it when it was about 40 cents – and now it's in the range of $800.

"The problem is that it doesn't operate as a store of value, unlike, say, gold," he said. "This is my beef with the whole bitcoin vs. gold argument."

Robinson brings onto his program Trace Mayer, who has produced the ebook "Bitcoin Beginner's Guide."

"This is not going to end well for those who are buying at these levels," Robinson suggested. "Could it go higher? It could. Much higher. But I think it's going to be boom, bust, boom, bust."

He noted that there now are numerous "bitcoin wannabes" out there.

"It's all a bubble, designed to get your eye off the ball," Robinson said.

Jerry Robinson also said a bitcoin is "strictly for speculative money."

Jerry Robinson is just one of many Bitcoin non-believers out there. However, all of the non-believers that aren't in Bitcoin – are they losing out on vast opportunities for major profit in trading?

According to the chart, one can see the rise from Bitcoin from relative obscurity. It happened very fast.

Here's what Bitcoin has been valued at in the year 2012:

January 1, 2012	$5.17
February 1, 2012	$5.50
March 1, 2012	$4.55
April 1, 2012	$4.83
May 1, 2012	$5.01
June 1, 2012	$5.25
July 1, 2012	$6.64
August 1, 2012	$9.55
September 1, 2012	$9.92
October 1, 2012	$12.45
November 1, 2012	$10.60
December 1, 2012	$12.60

Now, take a look at what Bitcoin has been valued in 2013:

January 1, 2013	$13.25
February 1, 2013	$20.20
March 1, 2013	$34.50
April 1, 2013	$93.00
May 1, 2013	$115.00
June 1, 2013	$129.11
July 1, 2013	$88.13
August 1, 2013	$104.22
September 1, 2013	$144.24
October 1, 2013	$140.11
November 1, 2013	$212.50
December 1, 2013	$1211.15

Now – many will look at that chart and say, "Holy crap! Look at all the money that I could have made!" – And the fact is, Bitcoin may continue to go up even further from here.

In fact, if you looked at the chart of Bitcoin from 2010 and 2011 – Bitcoin was worth even less than $1.00!

So what exactly is the problem? Why aren't more and more people jumping into Bitcoin and turning each Bitcoin into more and more money? After all – it seems to have all the relative qualifications for a viable currency. Only 21,000,000 Bitcoins can be created.

The problem is that the Booms and Busts will continue until someone will be "holding the bag" at the end of the day. And when Bitcoin fully matures and people decide they don't want it any more – then what?

That is the basis for concern for the creation of Bitcoin in the 1st place. If you go back to Chapter 2, Bitcoin has the ability to adapt and amongst it's members. Maybe Bitcoin will revolutionize the way money works into the next century – maybe Bitcoin is the "pioneer" of currency in today's generation.

The question is, "How much faith would you have in Bitcoin?"

If Bitcoin can turn it's form of currency mainstream, then it's possible that it will be competing with the Federal Reserve and other central banks to dominate the money market.

Maybe you should ask yourself, "How much faith do I have in this fiat currency dollar bill?"

There are many other pundits out there, other than Jerry Robinson who say, "Be careful" with your money.

According Eric Posner of Slate Magazine, Bitcoin is a fantasy.

(Source: http://www.slate.com/articles/news_and_politics/view_from_chicago/2013/04/bitcoin_is_a_ponzi_scheme_the_internet_currency_will_collapse.html#return)

Bitcoin is a Ponzi scheme—the Internet's favorite currency will collapse.

By Eric Posner

Bitcoin is not the first unregulated or private currency

Photo by Sean Gallup/Getty Images

Bitcoin is a fantasy. The Internet's currency—a secure, private, decentralized type of money that makes possible anonymous and virtually costless transactions across borders—contains the seeds of its own destruction. More than anything else, it resembles a Ponzi scheme—and the wild claims made on its behalf reveal a great deal about a libertarian strain of thinking with deep roots in the American psyche.

As Farhad Manjoo relates in his entertaining (but dubious) foray into the market, bitcoin is the brainchild of a person (or persons) called Satoshi Nakamoto. Computer users can "mine" bitcoins by instructing their computers to solve complex problems generated by the bitcoin network. As more bitcoins are produced, the problems become more complex, requiring more computer power to solve them, and this limits the total number of bitcoins that can be created over time. Bitcoins are themselves simply strings of numbers. Once you own a bitcoin, you can transfer it to someone else (as a gift or to purchase goods) over the Internet. You can also convert it into dollars or other currencies on various exchanges. The Bitcoin network keeps track of where the bitcoins are located, so you cannot spend a single bitcoin over and over again by trying to transmit the identical code.*

The currency was launched in 2009. It has traded for less than 1 cent. As recently as a year ago, a bitcoin was worth less than $5; this week the price of a bitcoin reached $266, an increase of more than 1,000 percent over the last three months, but then yesterday plunged to $105 before finishing off at $165 last I looked. More than 11 million bitcoins circulate, and so their aggregate value is fluctuating between $1 and $2 billion—a tiny fraction of the trillions of dollars in currency but not bad for the infant brainchild of an anonymous brain.

Bitcoin may be useful for certain types of transactions, especially illegal ones. But bitcoin's defenders argue that the experiment has proved that a currency can come into existence and function without any government role, so designed as to make inflation impossible and bank transfer fees unnecessary. These features are supposed to make bitcoins irresistible for

81

consumers. Meanwhile, stripped of the power to manipulate currencies to advance nefarious ends, governments will collapse, and we will live in an anarcho-utopia.

This is wrong, both theory and experience tell us. Bitcoin is not the first unregulated or private currency. Until central banks were invented in the 17th century, the money supply was unregulated even if governments did stamp coins. Other unregulated or private currencies have emerged from time to time—think of cigarettes in prison camps. Gold, silver, bank notes, and all kinds of other things have played similar roles. Paul Krugman wrote a famous *Slate* piece about a private currency that was invented to facilitate the exchange of services in a baby-sitting co-op.

Felix Salmon and many others have pointed out that a currency cannot succeed with a supply that is fixed, or if it grows too slowly. A currency is used to enter transactions; the more transactions there are, the more of the money you need. As the economy grows, a fixed-supply currency becomes worth more in terms of goods and services, and people begin to hoard it— expecting that if they wait a little longer, they will be able to buy more. Once hoarding takes over, circulation ends, and with it the function of the currency. Hoarding accounts for the large increase in the value of bitcoins; hoarding also sank Krugman's baby-sitting scrip.

An even more fundamental problem with bitcoins, and indeed any private currency, is that there is no way to limit its supply. True, bitcoins cannot be manufactured beyond the limits set by Nakamoto. But there is no way to prevent future Nakamotos from creating bitcoin substitutes—say, bytecoin, or botcoin. If merchants are willing to accept bitcoins, they will be willing to accept the substitutes, especially as bitcoins become scarce and consumers scramble for substitutes. Nakamoto must have realized this because there are not enough bitcoins to substitute for the currencies around the world. The currency can only succeed if it is expanded or supplemented. But if there are no constraints on substitute digital currencies—and there aren't—then the value of bitcoins will plummet as the subs begin to circulate. And once it becomes clear that there is no limit, people will realize that their holdings could become worthless at any moment, and demand for bitcoins and the other currencies will collapse, ending the experiment.

Unless a bitcoin has value as a currency, it has no value at all, and its price in dollars will fall to zero. A regular Ponzi scheme collapses when people realize that earlier investors are being paid out of the investments of later investors rather than from the returns on an underlying asset. Bitcoin will collapse when people realize that it can't survive as a currency because of its built-in deflationary features, or because of the emergence of bytecoins, or both. A real Ponzi scheme takes fraud; bitcoin, by contrast, seems more like a collective delusion.

Given this, why all the enthusiasm for bitcoin? Partly, the technological ingenuity of the scheme, of course. And people have misinterpreted the run-up in price as a sign of success rather than failure. But more fundamentally, bitcoin unites futuristic left-wing Internet anarchism—the fantasy that the Web can provide the conditions for a governmentless society—with the cave-dwelling right-wing libertarianism of goldbugs who think a stable money supply can be established without government involvement. It is proof for both that government is not needed for much, or at all.

Yet history shows that private currencies always end in tears; if central banks sometimes abuse the trust we place in them, the alternatives are worse. The strangest feature of the bitcoin saga is that people who are so suspicious of government put their trust in Satoshi Nakamoto, who could be anyone, or anyones—eccentric academic researchers, mischievous Fed economists, DARPA, U.N. globalizers in black helicopters, a criminal syndicate, a bored 11-year-old Ukrainian genius. If Nakamoto is as amoral as he is ingenious, then he pocketed the early bitcoins and laughed himself to the bank.

(Source: http://www.slate.com/articles/news_and_politics/view_from_chicago/2013/04/bitcoin_is_a_ponzi_scheme_the_internet_currency_will_collapse.html#return)

Currently Bitcoin is in the "BOOM" phase. Many of the articles quoted are based on speculation…. Is the "BUST phase next?

Chapter 7 – Perception vs. Reality

Bitcoin is moving in grand fashion at the end of 2013. Is the perception – that Bitcoin will lead the market place for a new type of currency – accurate?

This according to Alex Hern of Business Insider, dated November 26, 2013:

(Source: http://www.businessinsider.com/is-bitcoin-about-to-change-the-world-2013-11)

The past weeks have seen a surprising meeting of minds between chairman of the US Federal Reserve Ben Bernanke, the Bank of England, the Olympic-rowing and Zuckerberg-bothering Winklevoss twins, and the US Department of Homeland Security. The connection? All have decided it's time to take Bitcoin seriously.

Until now, what pundits called in a rolling-eye fashion "the new peer-to-peer cryptocurrency" had been seen just as a digital form of gold, with all the associated speculation, stake-claiming and even "mining"; perfect for the digital wild west of the internet, but no use for real transactions.

Bitcoins are mined by computers solving fiendishly hard mathematical problems. The "coin" doesn't exist physically: it is a virtual currency that exists only as a computer file. No one computer controls the currency. A network keeps track of all transactions made using Bitcoins but it doesn't know what they were used for – just the ID of the computer "wallet" they move from and to.

Right now the currency is tricky to use, both in terms of the technological nous required to actually acquire Bitcoins, and finding somewhere to spend them. To get them, you have to first set up a wallet, probably online at a site such as Blockchain.info, and then pay someone hard currency to get them to transfer the coins into that wallet.

A Bitcoin payment address is a short string of random characters, and if used carefully, it's possible to make transactions anonymously. That's what made it the currency of choice for sites such as the Silk Road and Black Market Reloaded, which let users buy drugs anonymously over the internet. It also makes it very hard to tax transactions, despite the best efforts of countries such as Germany, which in August declared that Bitcoin was "private money" in which transactions should be taxed as normal.

It doesn't have all the advantages of cash, though the fact you can't forge it is a definite plus: Bitcoin is "peer-to-peer" and every coin "spent" is authenticated with the network. Thus you can't spend the same coin in two different places. (But nor can you spend it without an internet connection.) You don't have to spend whole Bitcoins: each one can be split into 100m pieces (each known as a satoshi), and spent separately.

Although most people have now vaguely heard of Bitcoin, you're unlikely to find someone outside the tech community who really understands it in detail, let alone accepts it as payment. Nobody knows who invented it; its pseudonymous creator, Satoshi Nakamoto, hasn't come forward. He or she may not even be Japanese but certainly knows a lot about cryptography, economics and computing.

It was first presented in November 2008 in an academic paper shared with a cryptography mailing list. It caught the attention of that community but took years to take off as a niche transaction tool. The first Bitcoin boom and bust came in 2011, and signalled that it had caught the attention of enough people for real money to get involved – but also posed the question of whether it could ever be more than a novelty.

The algorithm for mining Bitcoins means the number in circulation will never exceed 21m and this limit will be reached in around 2140. Already 57% of all Bitcoins have been created; by 2017, 75% will have been. If you tried to create a Bitcoin in 2141, every other computer on the network would reject it as fake because it would not have been made according to the rules of currency.

The number of companies taking Bitcoin payments is increasing from a small base, and a few payment processors such as Atlanta-based Bitpay are making real money from the currency. But it's difficult to get accurate numbers on conventional transactions, and it still seems that the most popular uses of Bitcoins are buying drugs in the shadier parts of the internet, as people did on the Silk Road website, and buying the currency in the hope that in a few weeks' time you will be able to sell it at a profit.

This is remarkable because there's no fundamental reason why Bitcoin should have any value at all. The only reason people are willing to pay money for the currency is because other people are willing to as well. (Try not to think about it too hard.) Now, though, sensible economists are saying that Bitcoin might become part of our future economy. That's quite a shift from October last year, when the European Central Bank said that Bitcoin was "characteristic of a Ponzi [pyramid] scheme". This month, the Chicago Federal Reserve commented that the currency was "a remarkable conceptual and technical achievement, which may well be used by existing financial institutions (which could issue their own bitcoins) or even by governments themselves".

It might not sound thrilling. But for a central banker, that's like yelling "BITCOIIINNNN!" from the rooftops. And Bernanke, in a carefully dull letter to the US Senate committee on Homeland Security, said that when it came to virtual currencies (read: Bitcoin), the US Federal Reserve had "ongoing initiatives" to "identify additional areas of … concern that require heightened attention by the banking organisations we supervise".

In other words, Bernanke is ready to make Bitcoin part of US currency regulation – the key step towards legitimacy.

Most reporting about Bitcoin until now has been of its extraordinary price ramp – from a low of $1 in 2011 to more than $900 earlier this month. That massive increase has sparked a classic speculative rush, with more and more people hoping to get a piece of the pie by buying and then selling Bitcoins. Others are investing thousands of pounds in custom "mining rigs", computers specially built to solve the mathematical problems necessary to confirm a Bitcoin transaction.

88

But bubbles can burst: in 2011 it went from $33 to $1. The day after hitting that $900 high, Bitcoin's value halved on MtGox, the biggest exchange. Then it rose again.

Speculative bubbles happen everywhere, though, from stock markets to Beanie Babies. All that's needed is enough people who think that they are the smart money, and that everyone else is sufficiently stupid to buy from them. But the Bitcoin bubbles tell us as much about the usefulness of the currency itself as the tulip mania of 17th century Holland did about flower-arranging.

History does provide some lessons. While the Dutch were selling single tulip bulbs for 10 times a craftsman's annual income, the British were panicking about their own economic crisis. The silver coinage that had been the basis of the national economy for centuries was rapidly becoming unfit for purpose: it was constrained in supply and too easy to forge. The economy was taking on the features of a modern capitalist state, and the currency simply couldn't catch up.

Describing the problem Britain faced then, David Birch, a consultant specialising in electronic transactions, says: "We had a problem in matching the nature of the economy to the nature of the money we used." Birch has been talking about electronic money for over two decades and is convinced that we find ourselves on the edge of the same shift that occurred 400 years ago.

The cause of that shift is the internet, because even though you might want to, you can't use cash – untraceable, no-fee-charged cash – online. Existing payment systems such as PayPal and credit cards demand a cut. So for individuals looking for a digital equivalent of cash – no middleman, quick, easy – Bitcoin looks pretty good.

In 1613, as people looked for a replacement for silver, Birch says, "we might have been saying 'the idea of tulip bulbs as an asset class looks pretty good, but this central bank nonsense will never catch on.' We knew we needed a change, but we couldn't tell which made sense." Back then, the currency crisis was solved with the introduction first of Isaac Newton's Royal Mint ("official" silver and gold) and later with the creation of the Bank of England ("official" paper money that could in theory be swapped for official silver or gold).

And now? Bitcoin offers unprecedented flexibility compared with what has gone before. "Some people in the mid-90s asked: 'Why do we need the web when we have AOL and CompuServe?'" says Mike Hearn, who works on the programs that underpin Bitcoin. "And so now people ask the same of Bitcoin. The web came to dominate because it was flexible and open, so anyone could take part, innovate and build interesting applications like YouTube, Facebook or Wikipedia, none of which would have ever happened on the AOL platform. I think the same will be true of Bitcoin."

For a small (but vocal) group in the US, Bitcoin represents the next best alternative to the gold standard, the 19th-century conception that money ought to be backed by precious metals rather than government printing presses and promises. This love of "hard money" is baked into Bitcoin itself, and is the reason why the owners who set computers to do the maths required to make the currency work are known as "miners", and is why the total supply of Bitcoin is capped.

And for Tyler and Cameron Winklevoss, the twins who sued Mark Zuckerberg (claiming he stole their idea for Facebook; the case was settled out of court), it's a handy vehicle for speculation. The two of them are setting up the "Winklevoss Bitcoin Trust", letting conventional investors gamble on the price of the currency.

Some of the hurdles left between Bitcoin and widespread adoption can be fixed. But until and unless Bitcoin develops a fully fledged banking system, some things that we take for granted with conventional money won't work.

Others are intrinsic to the currency. At some point in the early 22nd century, the last Bitcoin will be generated. Long before that, the creation of new coins will have dropped to near-zero. And through the next 100 or so years, it will follow an economic path laid out by "Nakomoto" in 2009 – a path that rejects the consensus view of modern economics that management by a central bank is beneficial. For some, that means Bitcoin can never achieve ubiquity. "Economies perform better when they have managed monetary policies," the Bank of England's chief cashier, Chris Salmon, said at an event to discuss Bitcoin last week. "As a result, it will never be more than an alternative [to state-backed money]." To macroeconomists, Bitcoin isn't scary because it enables crime, or eases tax dodging. It's scary because a world where it's used for all transactions is one where the ability of a central bank to guide the economy is destroyed, by design.

For Bitcoin developer Hearn, that's not a concern. "Bitcoin's monetary policy would only be relevant if it were to be adopted by an entire economy, which isn't going to happen any time soon."

Already, alternatives based on Bitcoin have sprung up: for instance, Litecoin speeds up transaction processing and Freicoin introduces measures to stop people hoarding their money, but both are essentially the same technology, "forked" from the original. There's even nothing to stop a nation state declaring its own version of Bitcoin as legal tender.

So even if the currency of the future looks like Bitcoin, it might end up being a distant successor of the pioneer. "Is the technology of Bitcoin a window into the future?" asks Birch. "Yes. Is Bitcoin itself? No."

(Source: http://www.businessinsider.com/is-bitcoin-about-to-change-the-world-2013-11)

The perception of Bitcoin now is:

- Bitcoin will continue to go up in value.
- Winklevoss Bitcoin Trust
- Computer currency equivalent of the gold standard

The reality of Bitcoin is this:

- Bitcoin will go bust – or be controlled by the government and then go bust.
- Winklevoss Bitcoin Trust? Tell me your kidding!
- There is no comparable to the Gold Standard. It's either gold, or it's not gold. There's no room for fiat!

Chapter 8 – Libertarian Warning

Texas Congressman Ron Paul was a presidential candidate for the 2012 term. He lost, but he proved to be a fantastic teacher to millions of Americans for the promotion of peace, freedom and prosperity.

Here are some key topics that Ron Paul discussed on April 23, 2012 on Bloomberg News:

Ron Paul on whether he's concerned about the drop in gold:

"I am concerned about the erraticness of the dollar. The dollar is up, the dollar is down. We print a lot of dollars. The dollar gets devalued. That is really the concern. If people think the gold price up and down is a reflection of something wrong with gold, no, I say it is something wrong with the dollar. People have been expressing concerns over the past couple of months about gold, but compared to what?"

Compared to where gold went from when the Fed took over where it was $20 per ounce compared to what has happened in the past?...

"I remember in the 1970's when they finally allow people to own gold and it went from $35 to $200 rather rapidly, and then it lost 50%. Then it went up to $800.

To compare a couple of months or a couple of weeks and forget about a bull market in gold price in relationship to the dollar for 12 years. I would say the comparison is not an authentic comparison. What you have to look at is the inflation. Inflation is an increased supply of money.

Since 2008 they have quadrupled the supply of Federal Reserve credit and are buying $85 billion per month of treasury bills. At the same time last week they bought $60 billion. That is the inflation. That is the distortion of the market and that's why we're not getting economic growth."

On whether inflation or deflation is occurring right now:

"It depends on how you define it. Inflation is when you increase the supply of money. Bond prices go up. Stocks are going up. Housing prices are starting to go back up again. Education costs are going up, but the gross distortion is the effect that the inflation of the money does on the price of money and interest rates and how it causes economic problems and why you don't get economic growth.

You have to look at the malinvestment and destruction that occurs when you mess around with the price of money. It's not just the CPI because the CPI is not reliable. The government fudges that as well. They change the way they measure it. Free-market economists say it is going up about 8%. A lot of deception going on out there. I was just talking to someone on getting social security, they're not happy with the purchasing power of the dollar and you can't tell me there is no inflation."

On the real value of gold and what it should be:

"No one knows it other than what is happening at that moment. The Supply and demand of gold is very important. That is why it is money, because gold is used elsewhere and it is commodity. The supply and money of paper is the culprit. That is the one that is causing all the trouble. People ignore the supply and demand of paper. Yes, paper goes up and goes down, but look at the long term purchasing power of the dollar. It has been devastating. At the rate they are printing the money, you will see a continual devastation of the value of the dollar."

"You will not see economic growth until you liquidate the debt and liquidate the malinvestment out there. Sure, you will see housing go up again, but you will see more bubble formation because prices go up does not mean there is economic growth. We are a long way from the correction, mainly because they ignore the definition of inflation and ignore the need to liquidate debt and the need to liquidate and get rid of all the malinvestment."

"One good comparison is look at the price of stocks and gold. Although in the past couple of weeks it has changed a bit. The price of the stock market has crashed, because you used to be able to buy the Dow with 44 ounces of gold. Now it is under 10 ounces of gold. It will probably go a lot lower."

"I think the way gold is acting it acts like a market does. You get ahead of itself, there has to be a correction. The amazing thing is not the correction, the amazing thing is the biggest bull market of the century when one commodity went up for 12 years straight. You cannot ignore that. To say, well there has to be an adjustment because prices are subjectively decided by many factors so you cannot predict exactly where the money will go. Unfortunately right now the money that the Fed creates goes into reserves, further distorting the markets and pumping up prices of bonds, further building a bubble that will burst because our economic growth is not there and we are in every bit as much trouble of Europe and Greece.

Someday there will be a lack of confidence in our dollar and you will see the correction in the paper a lot more severe than you see the correction in the dollar-gold ratio."

On Bitcoin:

"To tell you the truth, it's little bit too complicated. **If I can't put it in my pocket, I have some reservations about that.** But it has been designed in the free market. If it is a means of exchange, it would not ever be illegal. You shouldn't regulate it in the free market, but I do not think it fits the definition of money, which has been around for 6000 years.

People want to see something they can know what it is, they can define it, touch it and put in their pocket. If you do not have a computer and someone running the computer and calculations, you don't have it. I am not a big supporter of that, but I am not opposed to it. I admit, I do not fully understand what is going on with it."

Let's highlight a few key points of that interview with Ron Paul:

1. "One good comparison is look at the price of stocks and gold. Although in the past couple of weeks it has changed a bit. The price of the stock market has crashed, because you used to be able to buy the Dow with 44 ounces of gold. Now it is under 10 ounces of gold. It will probably go a lot lower."

Ron Paul blasted the Federal Reserve and the central banks because they have depreciated the value of the American dollar and limited its purchasing power.

2. "If I can't put it in my pocket, I have some reservations about that. I do not think it fits the definition of money, which has been around for 6,000 years. People want to see something they can know what it is, they can define it, touch it and put it in their pocket."

Ron Paul clearly understands the dynamics of money. He has written over 20 books, many of them on economic policy.

Here are some books authored by Ron Paul:

A Republic, If You Can Keep It

Challenge to Liberty

Gold, Peace, and Prosperity

Mises and Austrian Economics: A Personal View

Ten Myths About Paper Money

The Case for Gold

Freedom Under Siege: The U.S. Constitution After 200 Years

A Foreign Policy of Freedom

The Revolution

Abortion and liberty

Ron Paul speaks

The Revolution: A Manifesto

A Foreign Policy of Freedom: Peace, Commerce, and Honest Friendship

End the Fed

Liberty Defined

As you can see by simply looking at the titles of the books, it's obvious that Ron Paul knows exactly what he's talking about when it comes to economic and monetary policy.

History has also been on his side as he's showcased for over 50 years the fallacy of fiat currencies. The ol' Paper Tiger is on its way out.

Bitcoin has spurred an electronic money revolution. Have the impacts of Bitcoin all been negative? No. Many would argue that Bitcoin has opened up the opportunity for competing currencies.

Will Bitcoin be worth more than an ounce of gold in 2014? It's possible.

Will Bitcoin be worth more than an ounce of gold in 2015? Again – it's possible, but is it likely?

At the rate technology is changing, there is no doubt that there will be multiple other electronic currencies cropping up for consumer's to put their faith and trust in.

And that's just the point, the value of the American Dollar is currently based on the "full faith and credit" of the United States. What happens when that full faith goes KAPUTZ?

Bitcoin – and other digital forms of money – will continue to be around. Maybe Bitcoin is showing the timeline of the destruction of the dollar?

Here's one final article that showcases the path of Bitcoin:

Is It Time To Dump Your Gold And Buy Bitcoins?

Friday November 29, 2013 16:25

Have you thought about buying bitcoins this week? If so, you probably aren't the only one. After all, the surging price of bitcoins has been making headlines. The virtual currency skyrocketed to a new all-time high Friday at $1,242—after climbing above the $1,000 mark for the first time ever earlier in the week. Can anyone say panicked buying?

By one count, the value surged 24% on an intraweek basis, though values can vary from exchange to exchange. A few of the exchanges out there include the Toyko-based Mt. Gox, the Slovenia-based Bitstamp and The CoinDesk index is another source for pricing.

Bitcoins are now four years old and the increasing headline news, Congressional inquiries and rising prices begs the question—are bitcoins forming a bubble? And, for gold investors, a more important question lies at hand—have bitcoins replaced gold?

Is it time to dump your gold and buy bitcoins? Probably not. When it comes to the virtual currency there are several reasons to listen to the sage advice: Caveat Emptor, or "buyer beware."

Markets tend to "peak out" or post "blow-off" tops not long after the man on the street starts rushing to join the party. Remember the dot.com bubble implosion and subsequent U.S. stock market collapse in 2000-2002? The old joke is once your taxi driver starts giving you stock tips—look out a top is in the works. Why is that?

Markets accelerate in phases, fueled by different groups of investors. Generally the "smart money" gets involved in trends early. And, it is the "public" that rushes in at the end of a market-run fueling a late trend surge, which can form a "blow-off" top.

At tops the general public comes in because they are attracted to rising prices and good news. The general principles that underlie the markets don't change and continue to drive price cycles over and over again.

Beyond the issue of a speculative run-up, which could lead to a blow-off top and subsequent hefty downside correction in the value of bitcoins, there are other "issues" to consider.

Physical gold offers investors a tangible investment—a physical bar or coin to put in your safe deposit box, bury in your backyard. Bitcoins have no physical form.

Can anyone say hard drive crash!? Beyond that, this is a computerized technical system with who knows what vulnerabilities yet to be discovered.

Regulation ahead? Governments are sniffing around and getting interested in this virtual currency. The main attraction of no tracking, no taxation, or even government's inability to freeze someone's bitcoin assets could change.

Bitcoins may be here to stay, or just a passing fad. Only time will tell.

Gold investors have the backing of thousands of years of global history of using the metal as a currency, store of value and an investment—and that likely isn't going away anytime soon.

By Kira Brecht, Kitco.com

(Source: http://www.kitco.com/ind/Brecht/2013-11-29-Is-It-Time-To-Dump-Your-Gold-And-Buy-Bitcoins.html)

Once again, another author strikes home the point that hinges on success of a currency. Governments don't like competing currency.

Ben Bernanke, in a way, validated Bitcoin. When he did, the value of Bitcoin skyrocketed. Is it a policy of, "If you can't beat em', join em'"? Possibly.

The United States has lived beyond its means for many years. A national debt of over $16,000,000,000,000 – yes, that's TRILLION – is proof of that.

How much longer will consumers put their full faith and trust in the value of the dollar? Could those same consumers take that full faith in the value of a Bitcoin?

Nobody knows the future but one thing that is absolutely positively true – you can't make something out of nothing. For that reason alone, Bitcoin – like hundreds of other paper currencies – will fail.

If you value your hard earned money and want to make money like millions of others, maybe it would be a good idea to read more economic books. Start with the list that was given on page 96.

Otherwise, when the time comes and

Bitcoin goes KABOOM!

you might be the one who is holding the bag. Nobody wants to lose their financial stability. Ask the Dutch from Tulip Mania.

Caveat Emptor means
"Let the Buyer Beware!"

www.ingramcontent.com/pod-product-compliance
Lightning Source LLC
Chambersburg PA
CBHW051731170526
45167CB00002B/889